SCOTTISH MOUNTAINS ON SKI Vol. I

A

WEST COL SKIING GUIDES

Scottish Mountains
ON SKI

CLIMBS AND TOURS FOR WINTER & SPRING

44 route maps and eight plates

VOLUME ONE

Malcolm Slesser

West Col Productions

Scottish Mountains on Ski Vol I

First published in Great Britain 1970 by
West Col Productions
1 Meadow Close, Goring, Reading, Berks. RG8 0AP

SBN 901516 29 5

Printed in Great Britain by
The Kilburn Press Limited, Wallingford, Berkshire.

Contents

Contents

by JOHN WILSON

Preface

To the dedicated piste skier, the far side of the hill just isn't there. However there has been, always, a band of enquiring souls to whom the untracked back of the hill gives greater delight. This band increases all the time and the present book is going to accelerate the process.

What puzzles me is how Malcolm Slesser found the time to cover all the routes described. After all, he has a full-time academic post, is a dedicated practising mountaineer, a socialite and charming host, a political debater of ability, and a complete family man forebye. And in *all* these things he is an enthusiast, but never more than as a skier. It is hardly surprising then that some of the enthusiasm rubs off on to the descriptions — in fact, his own favourite discoveries come through with all the original charm and clarity of basic exploration.

Happily, his list is not exhaustive — happily, because we can hope for a companion volume. But, exhaustive or not, there is enough here to satisfy the most ardent and vigorous of ski-tourers for many a season!

Dunblane, Perthshire
July 1970

Introduction

This is not just a book for experts. It is a book for everyone who wants to go beyond the piste.

According to the Scottish Mountaineering Club, there are 544 mountains in Scotland above 3000 feet, and many more of lower height. Every one of them may be ascended by ski given just the right conditions. The purpose of this book is to guide the would-be mountain skier towards those summits which not only are worth skiing on, but which are also sufficiently accessible and which retain snow cover during periods of thaw.

The number of people skiing in Scotland is rising every year as is also their skill in performance. Already the ski-lift facilities available are swamped. With each season queues lengthen. Each season adds to the number of people who could ski off the piste. Each season the number tempted off the piste increases. But always there are the unknown factors; danger of avalanche, route-finding, more difficult snow. The police warning notices urge everyone to keep to the crowded slopes. Yet a whole new world is lying beyond, a world in which there are no crowds, no noise, no queues, but the opportunity to ski a virgin trail, to be oneself. It is a curious fact that the ascent of a mountain followed by the descent of a mere two and a half thousand feet, roughly equal to two and a half times a major descent by a Cairngorm or Glencoe tow, is more satisfying than a whole day spent piste-bashing during which one might knock up twenty or twenty-five thousand feet of downhill running.

Amongst the older generation there may be the view that mountain skiing and piste skiing are two different sports, appealing to different types of people and calling for different equipment. I cannot agree. Conditions are so rarely suitable for langlauf skiing — the skiing that we have come to associate with Scandinavia, rolling land, with deep blanket snow — that practically all off-piste skiing is mountain skiing. To do it well requires much more ability than to ski on a piste. To do it at all requires no great possession of skill, provided one chooses one's terrain. Nevertheless the more able one is upon the piste the greater the fun that can be extracted from a descent on the virgin snow slopes of a chosen mountain. Moreover fast mountain skiing calls for very precise control — the sort of control only provided by a good pair of downhill skis fitted with good bindings and using firm boots. The two activities are complementary, and can be exchanged one for the other on any day one has the urge, without change of equipment.

UNDERSTANDING SCOTTISH SNOW CONDITIONS

It is a fact that both skiers and climbers have been caught in avalanches in Scotland. The occasions have been rare, and the risk is nothing like so high as in the Alps because the sun angle is rarely so high, and the climatic cycles are different. Nevertheless one should learn to assess the risk. In this guide the routes have been classified, and those in categories 1 and 3 are unlikely ever to present avalanche risk.

Avalanches are complex things, still imperfectly understood. One can more easily predict their likelihood on a given slope when one knows the previous weather pattern. If there has been a thaw, then frost, the surface will be hard. If snow falls on top of this to any great depth, there will be a period during which it has very little adhesion to the underlying surface. A sonic bang or a traversing ski may be enough to set off movement that takes away the whole slope. If a moist wind has been blowing it is possible that wind crust (wind-slab) may form on lee sides of hills. This is very dangerous. When the avalanche starts the snow breaks into box like slabs, and woe-betide anyone caught in the avalanche.

Safe snow may avalanche just because it is very steep.

One can often ski quite safely in this sort of snow. In very cold powder snow the snow may spill out beneath one's skis, and run downhill carrying quite a weight of snow before it, without the slope itself collapsing. Equally in spring snow and warm weather one can ski down tremendously steep slopes almost riding on the mini-avalanches that one creates through each turn.

Avalanches are something one cannot learn about simply by reading, though as the bibliography indicates, there are books about them. One must gain experience. This is best obtained by travelling with someone more experienced; yet the ultimate safety is a good nose for mountains and slopes, and one can only learn this by trial and error experience. A wise precaution on a suspicious looking slope is to unclip the safety straps of the skis and take the hands out of the loops of the sticks. The great danger is that as one is carried down, the snow acting through one's skis will simply screw the whole body. With the above precautions the skis will be released by their safety bindings and then fall off.

To appreciate the potential for mountain skiing one must appreciate the vagaries of the Scottish climate. Even in the most arctic-alpine climate in the country, the Cairngorm plateau, every winter is a succession of freezes and thaws. Moreover, Scotland is a windy country. In the Alps the conditions are not so consistently windy, and the thaw, due to the high altitude, is rarer. Curiously it is the very climatic cycle that brings out the best in Scottish skiing. For by Spring the snow in the gullies will be highly compacted and of great depth. Coire na Ciste in the Cairngorms has sections in which a depth of 40 feet of snow is not unusual. The result is that such snow beds will outlast prolonged thaws, giving, in the cases mentioned, skiing in July.

The sort of alpine condition of blanket snow cover does occur, but is rare and generally confined to the month of February. It is true that a big all-over fall can occur any time from November onwards, but though the hills may appear totally white, six or eight inches of snow is not enough to form a basis for mountain skiing unless the mountain is grass clad. For this reason several such peaks are listed, for they are most useful in early season. In February it is not uncommon to have a good fall building up on ground in which the gullies and hollows are already well filled with compacted drifts. In such conditions almost any peak in Scotland can be skied upon. And in one year or another it is certain that all mainland peaks can offer skiing.

This pattern of thaw and freeze, may or may not be accompanied by snowfall. Thus for a mountain to be on our list it must have attributes that cause the snow to accumulate, and to outlast thaw periods. A factor here is the direction of the wind from which the snow has fallen. There may be a heavy fall from the North-West followed by a high wind from the South-East. If the thaw line is then around 1500 feet all the snow is simply blown over the tops down to the thaw lines, where it vanishes. The fall is wasted.

Snow in Scotland generally comes from the North-West or North-East, and both of these are cold winds. It also comes from the South-West, and though this wind is traditionally mild there are many times in the deep winter when it is cold enough to give freezing conditions on the upper parts of the mountains. Then it is an extremely good wind, creating massive build-up of snow in the gullies, broadening them, and extending the ski areas. Since our greatest corries face north, this results in deep collection in such corries, while at the same time southern faces get good overall cover.

There are many superb south facing slopes in the Scottish hills. Obviously as the spring advances and the sun strengthens, the snow on these slopes melts faster than on northerly slopes. Yet these are the best, because here one can enjoy the exquisite pleasures of sun and snow. It will be noted that no Scottish lifts operate on south facing slopes, and the skier wanting the real MacKay must go to the southern slopes on foot. In short he must ski-tour in order to enjoy the quintessence of the sport.

When frost follows a deep thaw without intervening snowfall the slopes will be hard. The popular pisted slopes are then like concrete — hopeless and dangerous. However, in these conditions the unpisted slopes can offer excellent skiing. The snow does not, as in the pistes, set like smooth concrete of the glacial kind, but freezes into a rippled form, like the sand at low tide, and stiff downhill skis can get a good grip. One can then travel very fast on snow which has the merit of being totally consistent. The danger, of course, lies where one has to cross steep slopes. A slip can bring an uncontrollable fall unless one has mastered the mountaineer's technique of arresting a fall on snow. Even so, there is a limit on how steep a slope one may check a fall. See the section on technique.

The most difficult snow is crusted snow, and it requires an expert in parallel skiing with great strength and stamina to make much of it. One would not choose to go mountain skiing in such conditions. Yet, one must not jump to any conclusions from one observation on the state of the snow. The cycle of temperatures that the snow has gone through, and which defines what the snow texture is, will vary with height. One may have concrete at 2000 feet, but exquisite powder on a firm base higher up because up there the thaw never took place. Remember that as a rule the temperature drops roughly 3 degrees for each thousand feet of ascent. One can use this rule to predict many things from the state of the surface to the likelihood of an avalanche due to thaw.

Finally, the tops of most Scottish hills over 2500 feet are rocky crests for the most part windswept. They can only be skied in high season — usually February and early March, when the uniquely damp, but freezing winds, will put a sheath of ice round each stone and then cover it with snow. The sharpest crest then shows no rock. But in early and late season the crests are out. In late season, however, the edge of the ridge, where cornices are formed, hold the snow and in spring may offer an excellent ribbon up to the highest tops and down by the lowest burn. Just beware of cornices. Such skiing on the top sections is strictly for precise controlled skiing.

EQUIPMENT

The short answer to the question — "Do I need special equipment?" is "No". And the long answer is that there are many refinements well worth having.

For the purposes of this book, ski-touring is regarded as mountain skiing. No ascents are described calling for long runs on flat ground, as there are few occasions when Scotland offers such opportunities. The refined way to ascend on skis is to use 'skins'. But they are not necessary to the person making his first investigations into the joys of mountain skiing. For one thing, skins work well only on consistent snow surfaces which are not hard. If the snow is hard one can undoubtedly walk faster than one can ski uphill even with skins. Furthermore the vagaries of the Scottish weather will mean that for the most part, except in high season or after a big fall, the ridges will be windswept and largely clear of snow, and one can walk up most summits. The important equipment to be considered is the equipment for descending, not for ascending.

EQUIPMENT FOR DESCENT

The first thing to be said is that it cannot be too good. The confirmed downhill man will in his early days of mountain skiing take old and battered skis that have seen their best days. Eventually he will take his newest and best.

SKIS

Any skis will do. The best skis are best. If selecting a pair of skis with mountain skiing specifically in mind one must accept that the demands of the uphill section are not totally compatible with those of the downhill section.

Langlauf skis are disappointing on the downhill, and rob this section of much of the excitement and joy of descent. Moreover in Scotland all over deep powder snow is too rare to justify them. Metal downhill skis are about the best one can have. Except under icy conditions one should avoid the very stiff reising slalom type, which do not flex to the contours of the terrain too well, and are apt to embed themselves on quite minor bumps to the detriment of the wearer. The lightweight CPM 70 type is excellent. Both types resist the Scottish weather satisfactorily. The short ski is a menace on the descent, for having a lower bearing surface area the pressure on the snow is increased, and the ski cuts further through the crust. Furthermore there is less fore and aft stability, and since off-the-piste skiing often means travelling through snow of differing surface friction, one can be thrown forwards and back as one moves from one snow texture to another. The longer ski affords much more security and stability. For maximum downhill enjoyment the usual long piste ski is desirable. If anything, the competent skier should go for a ski on the long rather than the short side, taking an extra 5 cm., and having the bindings placed as for slalom position.

The greatest joy in downhill mountain skiing is carving a turn through deep powder snow, and looking back on the trail, the only one on the hillside. Equipment should be chosen with this in mind. Every other snow texture can be handled so long as one has good boots, good edges and firm downhill bindings.

BINDINGS

The binding should offer both forward release and torsion release, since a fall in deep or crusted snow can be far more dangerous than on the piste. Release settings should be on the easy side.

OTHER EQUIPMENT

On the downhill run, as any downhill skier knows, one does not want one's hat to blow off, or rucksack to swing lazily about one's back. Everything should be tightly attached. In particular choose a rucksack that fits closely to the back, and which can be strapped at the waist. Cold can reduce effectiveness. One must leave the summit adequately dressed, particularly with respect to the hands.

EQUIPMENT FOR ASCENT

SKIS: If carrying the ski, the weight is important, but not critically so if a good carrier frame is used (see later). If skinning, the weight of the ski is most important. With heavy metal skis, the amount of weight to be pushed around puts a great strain on the thigh muscles. The lightest possible ski is desirable. Hence the development of the light Norwegian Langlauf ski, and the even lighter Finnish ski, though neither has much application here. A compromise can be obtained using a Norwegian Ash ski with metal edges.

However my recommendation is a high grade, light ski, of which the CPM 70 introduced in 1968 is an excellent example. Though short skis are easier to carry, and less weight, they are at a disadvantage, except on hard winter snow or firm spring snow.

BOOTS: The boots must not be of the super modern utterly rigid sort. But equally the traditional touring boot that was little more than a climbing boot with square toes and heel groove should be rejected since it reduces the control and pleasure of the descent. The best boots are those that can be comfortably roomy on the ascent, with a sole that flexes very slightly, but which on the descent can be quickly made extremely firm, holding the heel down. There are several excellent "touring boots" available today, though seldom for sale in Britain, comprising of an inner and outer, the inner being usable as a hut boot. Less expensive and more readily available are good quality single layer clip boots. Clips have the enormous advantage that in difficult conditions they are speedily adjustable, from uphill roominess to downhill firmness.

BINDINGS: It is not always realised by the person who has only skied downhill, that for flat or uphill skiing the binding must be of a type that allows the heel of the boot to rise. The old fashioned Kandahar binding, with large toe irons, and fore and aft side clips permitted this. By threading the cable through the rear side clips the boot was firmly held down for the downhill section. However, the degree of firmness was insufficient to meet the demands of better skiers, using better skis and firmer boots. Moreover the toe irons were fixed in position, so that there was no torsion release mechanism. Such bindings are today considered too dangerous for skiing. There are four current solutions to the problem, three of which involve adaptions of conventional downhill bindings —

1. *Heel Attachments:* For those who like the heel attachment as their forward release safety device, there is an adaption in which the heel fixture is attached to a flexible plate. On the uphill sections, the plate is free to rise as the boot rises. On the downhill section, a small clamping screw holds the plate firmly onto the ski. All in price about £12. It can be finicky to adjust, but is certainly very neat. One must step out of one's skis to effect the changeover. Another type — the Su-matic, allows the heel to rise over a limited height. It is very expensive. *Photo 1.*

2. *Cable Bindings:* This is an excellent dual-purpose type, falling out of favour with the downhill skier. There are fore and aft side clips, both in use for downhill running, but only the forward ones for uphill travel. The problem on the uphill position is that with the usual torsion release fixtures at the toe, the boot is not firmly enough held and slips out. This is remedied by fixing a 'clou', a small toe unit with adjustable side lugs attached to a plastic plate that is horizontally hinged at the heel position. For uphill

17

work the boot is held in position by the lugs. Either in uphill or downhill position it in no way impairs the torsion release action of the toe iron, which will probably be of 'Marker' or similar torsion release type. The 'clou' mates with the toe iron. With this type of binding one need not take off one's skis to change from uphill to downhill position. *Photos 2 and 3.*

3.   *Separate Attachment:* Some manufacturers sell a clip that fits over the ski at the toe iron, giving the same benefits as the 'clou'. Its drawbacks are that it needs fitting each time, it is separate and therefore can get lost, and it prevents torsion release. The last factor might not seem serious on the uphill section, but for those who anticipate any advanced mountain skiing in the Alps or on steep slopes in Scotland, there is always the possibility of a slip or an avalanche on the ascent. In such a situation it is desirable to have a torsion release.

4.   *Silvretta:* The ingenious Munich firm of Salewa has invented the almost perfect touring binding. It produces least wear on the toe of the boot, and requires very little adjustment from one boot to another. It is very lightweight, and uses the cable tension to draw side frames round the boot. It is hinged at the toe position. It is not quite so firm in the downhill position as one would wish and has no torsion release action. It is an excellent combination for expedition work, and well worth having on short skis, where the risks of torsion break are less.

STICKS: The modern downhill skier will use short sticks. They will be very light and have vestigial 'baskets'. For mountain skiing on the descent a short stick is still perfectly satisfactory, though a basket of about 4 inches in diameter is desirable. Lightness is a great asset.

However, on the ascent, there is no doubt that a long stick is useful, especially if the snow is deep and one is doing any traversing. Here is a problem that is hard to resolve. The short stick on the ascent can be very tiring on the arms and shoulders, yet on the descent the long stick tends to destroy one's downhill style, and therefore one's effectiveness and safety. A reasonable compromise is to take a stick that comes to within about four inches of one's armpits. It is useful if the straps are adjustable.

SKINS: Skins are strips of material with a sloping pile on one side laid on the ski so that when the ski slides forward it offers little resistance, but as the ski slides back, the pile springs out and grips the snow. Originally sealskin was used, and nothing better has yet been invented. Cost precludes their use. Today all skins are made of synthetic fibre, and the choice between them hinges largely on the type of fixing offered. It is false economy to go for a cheap pair as one is dealing with a price range of from £4 to £6.

The important features to look for are :—

1. Quick action fastening of main skin, preferably at the toe of the ski rather than the heel.
2. The side clips should be made of metal to resist abrasion. Most skins end their lives due to weakness here.

The skins should be fitted to the ski, for the position of the side clips will depend on the position and type of the bindings. As a test of usefulness, try to see whether with the skin on your skis, and your feet in the bindings you can take off the skins without taking off your skis. This facility is a most useful one when faced with a storm-swept mountain top, or a sudden decision to retreat while on a steep slope. One type that meets these standards is the 'Venersa'.

'Trima' skins have no side pieces, but lugs in the groove of the ski. From the point of view of ascent, they are the best available. This fitting has the unpleasant effect of slightly slowing down one's speed, which matters very much on gentle slopes. Otherwise they are excellent.

With snow at or just below freezing temperature the snow tends to get between the ski and the skin, creating balling up. This is minimised by having the skins stretched really tight, and avoiding skiing over any damp patches. This problem is minimised with 'Trima' skins.

A recent innovation is a skin which uses a mild adhesive. It is time consuming to put on the adhesive, but the system works well and avoids balling up. It is not a satisfactory method if skins are to be put on and off several times in one trip.

Finally, skins are essentially fitted to a given ski. One should not imagine that one can borrow or lend them. Try new skins out indoors before embarking on any trip.

CARRYING FRAME: Though in deep snow there is no satisfactory alternative to skins, there are many occasions when the snow is not deep, or the crests are blown clear or simply that the snow is a long way from the car, and a walk is needed. There are few activities less pleasant than carrying skis over one's shoulder, and half an hour of that is enough for most people. The solution is to have a carrying frame. There are a great many on the market. The best are the lightest, and vary in price from about £3 to £10. With a comfortable frame one can carry two pairs of skis and hardly notice the load. The American Alcan pack-frame is superb, and has a nice detachable strut that is tailor-made for supporting skis.

Putting skis through rucksacks is not terribly effective, and usually more nuisance than it is worth. However, there are some specially designed alpine rucksacks that take skis in a vertical position, and these are fairly satisfactory.

RUCKSACK: This must be close-fitting and have a waistband. If one of the party is taking a frame, another can take a sack to carry the spare clothing, food and safety equipment.

CLOTHES: For mountain skiing, one must have clothes suitable for the mountain. Modern ski garments are often too skimpy. Anoraks, for example, do not always come down over the backside, and the cloth may not be windproof.

20

However, the key thing is not to go out onto some exposed place from which one cannot quickly retreat, without both windproof trousers and a jacket with a hood, an ear-hugging hat, and woollen gloves with windproof outer. It is most unwise to use garments that are impermeable to water vapour, for this will result in sweat, and the destruction of the thermal insulating qualities of the inner clothing. A point to remember is that many modern textiles have shiny or smooth exteriors. This means they have minimal adherence to the snow surface, which is excellent from the point of view of elegance, but the worst possible thing from the point of view of safety. Winter mountaineers deliberately use hairy tweed trousers, for such things give an enormous grip on even quite steep icy snow. Many a skier would have been saved a nasty slide by wearing hairy breeks. The higher the grade of the projected ski climb, the more one should gravitate towards the mountaineer's rig.

SAFETY

Quite apart from the obvious and constantly voiced warnings that one should always carry a one inch to mile map, a compass and a whistle, and know how to use them, the mountain skier should recognise that his risks are somewhat different from those of the mountaineer on foot. On the one hand in good visibility, he can descend very fast. On the other he can break a limb on innocent ground which would never harm the mountaineer. It is important then to have safety bindings adjusted to release easily on a forward throw, and to have a torsion release binding. One should NEVER ski alone. The party should have amongst them sufficient emergency clothing to fit out at least one injured person if that person has to remain on the hill awaiting a rescue party. Always carry some emergency food and a change of socks and wool gloves. Always let someone know where you and where your party is heading. If you park a car in some remote spot, leave a note in the windscreen stating destination, and anticipated return time. Always put the date on the message.

TECHNIQUE FOR MOUNTAIN SKIING

This is not a book of technique. There are, however, a number of points worth special mention.

Of all the means of uphill locomotion on foot, skinning is the most pleasant. A satisfactory rhythm can be achieved very easily, and one can go on for hours. It is unlikely that any two people will have the same stride and rhythm, and one should be careful not to get so close to the person making the trail that one is forced to use his rhythm. It can quickly cause fatigue.

Skinning uphill on virgin soft snow gives a lot more work for the leader than the rest of the party. Moreover the angle of his skis will be slightly greater. It follows that if his skis do not slip back, everyone else's should get a good grip. The leader should be changed from time to time on a long ascent.

On the ascent consider the descent line. In the guide there are outline maps of each area, but these show only the route of ascent. This is partly to keep the diagrams simple, and partly because the best route of descent is variable depending on a particular season and the time of year.

If the weather is misty, and the route of descent is that of ascent, it pays to have the ascending party spread out to create parallel tracks ten yards apart. This will facilitate following the tracks of descent. If the weather is windy, stop below the summit and put on extra clothing so that on arrival one is already adequately dressed, and can turn one's whole attention to removing skins and preparing bindings and boots for the descent.

One finds that the hours of ascent accustom the body to a position quite foreign to that needed for a good downhill skiing. Even the best skiers tend to find themselves leaning too far back at the start of the descent. If conditions are misty or windy, this quickly results in 'defensive' skiing, with the unhappy result of frequent falls and lack of enjoyment. The first thing to do when one has all one's downhill system ready is to do a few tightly linked turns. No matter what the standard of the skier or the coarseness of the terrain, set off doing as tightly linked turns as possible, and then return to the summit to collect rucksack and other impedimenta.

Wax is a subject upon which the experts will argue for hours. My recommendation is to apply and smooth over Toko Yellow, and then apply over it Toko Blue. This may be done before leaving the valley. The blue wax provides an excellent running surface for new or powder snow. The moment the ski meets wet or spring snow the blue vanishes, and the yellow wax comes into operation. This sequence is useful since one often moves from frozen terrain downwards into thawing terrain.

At the summit after removing skins check that the running surface is free of nodules of ice and snow.

STOPPING A FALL

This technique is commonplace amongst climbers, and is made known in many textbooks (see Bibliography, Blackshaw). The climber using an ice-axe, grasps the head with one hand, putting his hand over the centre of it. He grasps the base of the shaft with his lower hand, and then pointing the pick downwards, lies upon the shaft. In this way he can stop himself sliding on quite steep and hard snow.

The skier is at a disadvantage. Both his hands are already occupied with sticks. Even if he has an ice-axe, he will not be able to reach it in time. When he falls, his skis tend to act as an anchor, so that within seconds he is falling downhill headfirst. The situation is potentially dangerous, but he would not expect to be in serious trouble unless he was involved in a route of category 4 or above.

The technique for stopping a fast slide is to let go the grip on one stick, and (with the hands still through the strap of that stick) grab the other stick as near the basket as possible and then lean on it, thus forcing the sharp tip of the ski-stick into the snow, and bracing the body against it, applying pressure. This will provide a greater breaking action than the skis, which will therefore remain below. Then by edging the skis, and continuing to dig the stick-point into the snow, the skier can come to a stop.

The problem is what to do next. If the slope is safe enough, his companions should ski down, and support him from beneath while he gets back on his feet. If not, and they have a rope, it should then be thrown down with a loop ready made. Make sure that a good belay stance has been created before trying any heroics. If there is neither rope nor a safe possibility of getting down to the skier, he should try to see whether he can bring his legs up, and then by running his edges to and fro, get a grip on the snow. It is not easy to do this. If he fails the people above will have to take action of some sort. The best hill man amongst them must take off his skis, and taking one stick, descend to the skier by kicking steps in the snow. Clearly the possession of an ice-axe and crampons would be of great help here, and for any route of category 5 or above the party should be carrying at least one axe, a 100 feet of light rope, and at least one pair of crampons. The same would apply if doing a category 4 route in conditions of hard or ice snow.

Tweed trousers represent a considerable safety factor when a fall occurs on steep hard snow!!

Here are a few general do's and dont's :—

1. If your descent takes you over steep or icy or rocky terrain, be sure to wear a hat.

2. On dangerous icy slopes, or if there is any avalanche danger, let one person try out the slope before the others cross. Remember that the standard of the party is the standard of the weakest skier.

3. If there is risk of avalanche, be sure to have safety straps undone, and hands out of the ski pole straps.

4. In dull lighting or in mist it is often impossible to distinguish up from down, a precipitous void from a safe slope. Move very carefully and do not hesitate to rope or to walk instead. A moving body ahead can be of immense help to those behind. Good lighting of the slope is one of the biggest safety factors on a virgin

slope. Bad lighting can be extremely dangerous, and can destroy the morale of even quite good skiers.

5. If your journey is higher than grade 3, be sure that all members in the party know how to use their ski sticks to stop a slip on steep snow.

6. If your route is grade 4 or above carry at least one ice-axe and a rope in the party.

7. Always leave a note of your intended destination and projected time of return.

8. In bad conditions, ski slowly.

USING THE GUIDE

There are several indexes designed to assist the user. In them the routes are correlated by :—

Index 1: Standard of route.
Index 2: Grouped by areas.
Index 3: Grouped by season in which likely to give good skiing.
Index 4: Alphabetical list of peaks, at end of book.

The data on each route is in the same order, and has the following significance :—

Character: The reference here is to the interest of the mountain, whether subtle or straightforward.

Season: The skiing season clearly varies from one year to another. The dates given here merely indicate those times at which one could normally expect to find skiing. However, some winters show negligible falls before January. Where an earlier date is indicated, it suggests that skiing is possible without a build up of snow.

Aspect: This applies to the route of descent, not ascent, and is helpful in deciding whether snow will be lying, and in what condition, a judgement which must be based on the past weather pattern.

Access: Not everyone has a car. Where a peak can be gained by a public bus service this is indicated. The criterion of accessibility is that one should not have to walk far with skis on one's back, and that in general one can ski back to near the car.

Amount of Climbing Involved (Ascent): Allows for any re-ascents along the route.

Altitude at end of Descent (Ter. alt.): Refers to end of descent on ski and foot.

Amount of Downhill Skiing (Downhill run): This figure assesses the lowest likely skiable snow line.

Time to Main Summit: The time taken to climb a peak in winter is very variable. Deep snow, crust, wind, or whether on foot or skins will all affect the timing. The times given are for reasonable conditions and for fit people of modest physique, not supermen.

Variations: These are often of greater difficulty, and one should consider the composition of the party before changing plan.

Traverse: A traverse implies that one finishes up somewhere different from the point of origin. Before embarking on a traverse make sure that arrangements have been made to be picked up, or that one has the necessary energy to get back to the car.

Diagram (Diag.): All routes have a diagram. These are no substitute for having a proper one inch to the mile map, and are there merely to clarify the written description. The route of ascent is shown in dotted lines. The route of descent is only shown where it is considerably different from the route of ascent. It is shown as a crossed trail.

Approach: The burgeoning tourist traffic in Scotland has resulted in the closing of more and more private glen roads. It is harder than it ever was to get off the main roads and into the hills except on foot. The mountain skier is fortunate in that he comes at a time when the tourist traffic is negligible, and landowners are at their most amiable. Many roads which are blocked by locked gates in the summer are open in winter. This does not imply a right to use them, and though in this guide many such roads are indicated, it is always up to the user to obtain permission. It is well to remember that during a thaw following a long frost the passage of a car over an unmetalled road can create tremendous damage, and the person at whose expense the road is maintained is entitled to be very angry and demand compensation.

Many access roads run to considerable height, and may drift in with snow. If they are private one has no right to a snow plough, nor to the free privilege of being dug out. There is an obligation to park one's car off the road, and leave room for a large vehicle to pass. Never move off the main road without a shovel. Snow tyres or chains are useful, and on occasion essential.

In the author's experience it is not difficult to get permission to use private glen roads in winter, and camping is often permitted where in summer it would be taboo. There are innumerable lodges and bothies that are used by the climbing fraternity that suit the mountain skier, and it is worth taking out membership of the Mountain Bothies Association, for a complete list of these howffs.

There are places, such as Derry Lodge and Invercauld in the southern Cairngorms, where access is virtually impossible due to the attitude of certain landowners. The situation here is so bad, that it seems inevitable that public pressure will in the end overcome it.

Route Categories

The category refers to the minimum ability of the skier needed to accomplish the route safely.

Routes in which one can turn at choice —

Category 1. Able to traverse and kick turn. Generally related to gentle terrain without danger of avalanche or slide.

2. Able to traverse, stem turn and side slip. Route carries risk of avalanche in certain conditions, and may in places under hard snow conditions carry risk of a slide in the event of a fall.

3. Moderate skiers accustomed to skiing in changing terrain and variable snow for several hours, but not to dealing with exposed or avalanche prone slopes.

4. Good skiers, or moderate skiers of strength; both with knowledge of mountains and route finding, able to check a slip on hard snow, and able to judge the safety of a slope.

Routes in which turning is dictated by the terrain —

5. Good skiers able to turn in restricted spaces, and able to do parallel turns in all types of of snow. Knowledge of mountains at least as good as 4, and able to judge the safety of snow slopes.

6. Good skiers able to do parallel turns in any snow in confined spaces who actively enjoy very steep ground, and who can confidently judge the safety of snow slopes.

Bibliography

Avalanche Enigma / Colin Fraser / John Murray
Mountaineering / Alan Blackshaw / Penguin Books
Mountain Rescue / HMSO 1968
On Foot and Ski in the Cairngorms / V. Firsoff / Robert Hale
Skiing in Scotland / Scottish Ski Club
SMC District Guides to / Scottish Mountaineering Trust / West Col Productions
  Southern Uplands / Andrews & Thrippleton, 1971
  Southern Highlands / Wilson, 1949
  Cairngorms / Alexander, 1968
  Central Highlands / Steven, 1968
  Northern Highlands / Strang, 1970
  Western Highlands / Parker, 1964
  Munro's Tables / ed. Donaldson & Coats, 1969

Abbreviations and Terms

Ascent	Vertical interval in feet from *dep. alt.* to summit or highest point of ski tour
Cat.	Category or degree of seriousness, skill, technique, difficulty involved in ski tour (see separate explanation)
Dep. alt.	Departure height above sea level, for ski tour
Diag.	Diagram cross reference, applied only to route descriptions which are combined in

	one diagram. Otherwise all route descriptions have an individual diagram.
Downhill run	Amount of downhill skiing, represented as the vertical fall in height
Map	Sheet numbers refer to the Ordnance Survey One-inch 7th series. Also Tourist Maps, quoted as alternatives, where available
R.	Route (cross reference)
Ter. alt.	Terminal height above sea level, at end of ski tour

Classified Index

1 Molls Cleuch Dod
2572 ft.

Character: *In the heart of a highly sculptured tableland of grass hills which catches all the snow going. Steep or gentle.*
Season: *Holds snow long after thaws. January to March.*
Aspect: *North-west.* **Access:** *Bus — none. Car — good. Moffat, Selkirk.* **Dep. alt:** 1141 *ft.* **Ter. alt:** 1141 *or* 711 *ft.* **Time to main summit:** 1½ *h.* **Cat:** 2, *but remote.* **Map:** *No.* 69.

Approach
Drive to the south-east end of Talla reservoir, lying between Tweedsmuir (A 701) and St. Mary's Loch (A 708).

Ascent Route
This depends on the snow conditions. If all over deep cover it is pleasant to skin up the north shoulder of Carlavin Hill, then along the summit ridge to Molls Cleuch Dod. If there is poor cover, or the skis are being carried, follow the track to Gameshope bothy on the burn of the same name that passes into the head of Talla reservoir.

Descent Route
The head of the Gameshope burn is a huge basin with many variants to be taken at choice. The south-east slope of Carlavin hill offers some steep ground, and if the sun has been acting over a few days it may give very firm and delightfully steep snow.

Variants
From Molls Cleuch one may continue with little climbing or descent to the hills at the head of the basin, such as Firthybrig Head (2504 ft.), Firthhope Rig (2627 ft.) and White Coomb (2696 ft.). All of these reduce the possibility of a direct descent back to the car without re-ascent or poling, but on a good day are well worth doing. The summit peat hags usually call for some route selection.

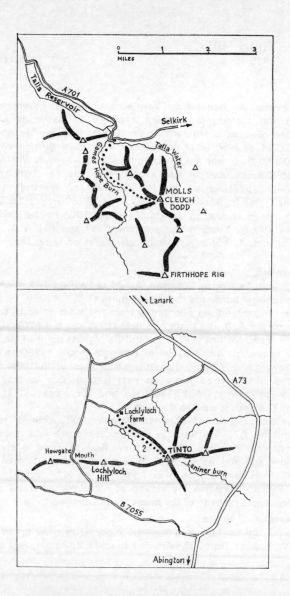

C

2   Tinto Hill
2335 ft.

Character: *An isolated but very accessible grass mountain in beautiful surroundings giving a choice of gentle or steep skiing.* **Season:** *Early, whenever 10 cm. of snow lies above 1000 ft. or high wind has created significant drifting above 1000 ft. Does not hold snow over a thaw.* **Aspect:** *North, or east.* **Access:** *Bus or car. Lanark.* **Dep. alt:** *(a) Lochlyock, 950 ft. (b) Howgate mouth, 1250 ft. (c) Westside (bus route), 795 ft.* **Ascent:** *(a) 1385 ft. (b) 1220 ft. (c) 1600 ft.* **Ter. alt:** *as at dep. alt.* **Downhill run:** *(a) 1385 ft. (b) 1550 ft. (c) 1550 ft.* **Time to main summit:** *(a) and (b), 1 h. (c), 1½ h.* **Cat:** *1, but enjoyable for all grades of skier.* **Map:** *No. 68.*

Approach

Bus from Lanark to Roberton. Alight at Feufield (A73) where the Lanimer burn cuts the road. (Route c).

Car: Recommended alternative from the west or north-west. Reach the A70 at Lanark or where it crosses the M74. If the side roads are not drifted in and the highest point of departure is sought, one may go to Howgate mouth (1250 ft.) by following the B7055 along the south side of the mountain till a narrow road leads up past a plantation to the gap between Howgate hill (1456 ft.) and Lochlyock hill (1735 ft.). The peak is now to the east.

The best ski run is obtained by going to Lochlyock farm. From the A70 the route is complex, for there is a maze of small country roads. But the N.W. flank of Tinto is always visible and acts as a guide. The simplest route is to take the A73 from Lanark (north) or Abington (on M74, south), and at Falburn opposite the village of Thankerton a road runs along the north side of the mountain to Lochlyock.

Selection of Route

(a)   From Lochlyock the gentle moor soon rises up to the N.W. spur of Tinto. The descent should hold to the west side,

34

but making for the spur because it consolidates faster than other parts of the mountain, and offers excellent steep skiing. If a gentler route is wanted, a zigzag on the Cleuch burn side will lead back to the moor.

(b) From Howgate mouth one must first ascend Lochlyock hill, ski down to 1600 ft., and take Tinto by the west ridge. The descent to Howgate mouth is gentle, and not satisfying to good skiers, who will be tempted to Lochlyock or Feufield.

(c) The upper part of Lanimer burn forms a steep corrie, and no matter the direction of the snow fall, will be filled in on one side. Several steep descents are available. Crags 800 ft. below the summit. The gentlest descent is obtained by either heading towards Lochlyock, and then doubling back on a long traverse below the steep ground, or from the summit going due east to the spur of Scout Hill (1924 ft.), whose east spur is not too steep. From its base one can reach the A73 (for a bus) or Feufield if a car is to be picked up.

Traverse
The ascent from Lochlyock and descent to the south-east is an excellent combination.

3   Cairnsmore of Carsphairn
(from S.E.)   2613 ft.   Kirkcudbrightshire

Moorbrock
2137 ft.

Character: *A fine isolated group of hills, of which Cairnsmore is the highest.* **Season:** *December to March.* **Aspect:** *Southeast.* **Access:** *Bus — none. Car — good. Nearest town, Moniaive.* **Dep. alt:** *1000 ft.* **Ascent:** *1600 ft.* **Ter. alt:** *600 ft. (traverse).* **Max. downhill run:** *2000 ft.* **Time to main summit:* 2 h.* **Cat:** 3. **Map:** *No. 67 (73 useful).*

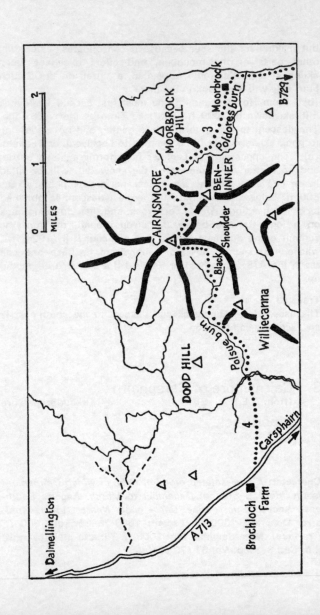

Approach

A metalled road strikes north from the B729 (Moniaive to Carsphairn) along the upper reaches of the Ken Water, serving a number of farms in that valley). At the first, Craigangillan, a track runs up the branch river, Pollferrie burn to Moorbrock farm (1000 ft.) Looking now to the N.W., the steep forms of Moorbrock (2137 ft.) and Beninner Gairy (2329 ft.) frame a shallow col which must be reached.

Ascent Route

Reach the col by the Poltie or Poldores burn. The Col (1500 ft.) is a boggy wasteland, obliterated, one hopes, with snow. From here a fine grass corrie leads east to Moorbrock hill (2137 ft.), while Cairnsmore rises very steeply to the west. According to the snow cover seen, choose either the steep gully between Beninner and the summit (bearing 230° true) or traverse on an upward track towards the north spur of the peak, which when gained, allows a return southwards to the summit along a broad shoulder.

Descent Route

Route of ascent.

Traverse

A series of successively lower hills fall to the S.W. of the summit. By following these — Black Shoulder (2258 ft.), Dunoal (1759 ft.), Williecanna (1300 ft.) one can regain the main road, A713 at Carsphairn (600 ft., Inn). Route ends on Map No. 73.

4 Cairnsmore of Carsphairn
(from west)   2613 ft.   Kirkcudbrightshire

Character: *A fine isolated group of hills.* **Season:** *December to March. Will hold snow longer than R.3 approach.* **Aspect:**

West. **Access:** *Bus — good, Car — good. Nearest town, Dalmellington.* **Dep. alt:** *(a)* 760 *ft.* (Brochloch), *(b)* 900 *ft.* **Ascent:** *(a)* 1950 *ft. (b)* 1700 *ft.* **Ter. alt:** 600 *ft., both.* **Max. downhill run:** 2000 *ft.* **Time to main summit:** *(a)* 2¾ *h. (b)* 2 *h.* **Cat:** 3. **Map:** *No.* 67. **Diag:** *R.*3.

Approach
(a) By bus, alight at Brochloch 2½ miles north of Carsphairn.

(b) By car, turn east off A713 half way between Carsphairn and Dalmellington (5 miles each way) at Lamford, where a farm road rises up through a gentle col. It branches, one striking north to serve several farms on Water of Deugh (e.g. Darnscow). Take the south branch as far as possible, probably to the ford on Water of Deugh. If this is in spate, it may be necessary to choose R.3.

Ascent Route
(a) From Brochloch farm, which lies on the west side of the road, take to the moor to the east. The summit can be seen just to the right of Dodd hill, which lies E.N.E. Do not aim for Dodd hill or the summit, but strike due east to meet the junction of Water of Deugh with the Polsue burn. This burn leads up to a shallow corrie between Cairnsmore and Black Shoulder (2258 ft.). Reach the shoulder, then ascend along the south ridge to the summit.

(b) The summit has been in view during the approach. Cross the Deugh burn and ascend on the north flank of Dodd hill making directly for the summit. The ascent is continuous, save for short easing at 1500 ft. Ahead now is the whole broad west face of the mountain, with the summit clearly visible.

Descent Route
Follow either route of ascent, or select the route of descent given in R.3.

Traverse
See R.3.

5   Corserine
2669 ft.   Kirkcudbrightshire

Character: *Highest point in a five mile ridge running north-south between desolate bogs of inner Galloway and the lush valley of the Ken. The lower slopes are shallow moor.* **Season:** *Upper slopes, December to March. Lower slopes according to season.* **Aspect:** *East.* **Access:** *Bus is possible, Car – good. New Galloway.* **Dep. alt:** *(a)* 650 *ft. (Bush Cottage). (b)* 737 *ft. (Bardennoch).* **Ascent:** *(a)* 2000 *ft. (b)* 2300 *ft.* **Ter. alt:** 650 *ft.* **Downhill run:** *(a)* 1900 *ft. (b)* 2200 *max.* **Time to main summit:** *(a)* 2½ *h. (b)* 3½ *h.* **Cat:** 3. **Map:** *No. 73.*

Approach
By bus (Ayr/Castle Douglas route), alight at Bardennoch, taking the track over the moor to Polmaddy burn and Castlemaddy. By car strike off the A713 (Castle Douglas/Ayr) road at Polharrow bridge at the north end of Earlston loch. A good metalled road runs along the south side of Polharrow burn to Forest Lodge, and on to Bush Cottage.

Ascent Route
(a)   From Bush follow the line of the burn towards Loch Harrow. Cross the burn before the loch and strike N.W. up steepening slopes into the Corrie that falls from the north side of North Gairy (2233 ft.).

(b)   From Castlemaddy cross the Polmaddy burn, and head on a contoured course towards North Gairy (2233 ft.), joining route (a).

The most skiable route lies upon the steep slopes on the north side of the corrie. At about 2000 ft. these ease off, and lead onto the spur running N.E. from the summit to Craigrine. This spur may not carry much snow during some seasons.

Descent Route
Route of ascent. Though the N.E. shoulder is broad enough to turn with ease there are cliffs each side. Beware of cor-

nices, and keep well away from the edge. In mist the route calls for great care. It frequently occurs that the S.E. corrie leading by the Hawse burn into Loch Dungeon holds snow, and since this corrie runs right to the summit of Corserine without any steepening near the top, it can provide a fine way off. Thus no matter what the ascent route, it is worth taking skis to the summit. The north side of the corrie is the least steep. Take care not to keep so high as to encounter the steep slopes under North Gairy, nor so low as to reach Loch Dungeon unless one is prepared to climb again to regain the car. Least effort is involved if, when about 500 ft. above Loch Dungeon, one heads for the north side of Loch Minnoch, from which a contour and a descent will lead to Bush.

Traverse

If there is excellent snow cover, those wishing to regain Bardennoch can ski along the summit ridge northwards till past the crags of Goat Craig, then to Cairnsgarroch (2155 ft.) and to Carsphairn village (600 ft., Inn).

For those with a car at Bush or Forest Lodge traverse south along the Rhinns of Kells to Meikle Millyea (2447 ft.). It is not easy to find a good way off here, and unless snow cover is good, the descent will be trying amongst heather and occasional rocks. Head for Loch Dungeon (steep section, some crags to avoid), and when below the crags of Mid Hill head for the Mid burn that runs directly to Forest Lodge via Burnhead cottage.

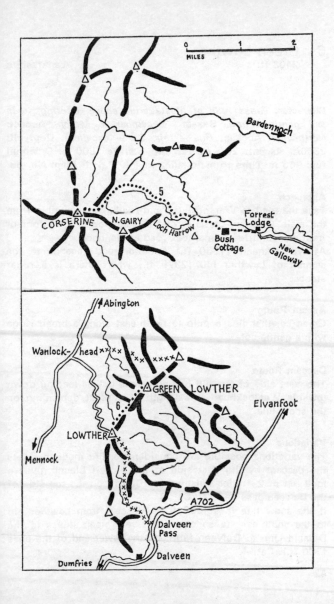

6 Green Lowther
2403 ft.

Character: *Grass hills of most varied shape, offering steep and gentle skiing.* **Season:** *December to March.* **Aspect:** *North-west.* **Access:** *Bus — fair, Car — excellent.* **Dep. alt:** *2300ft.* **Ascent:** *200 ft.* **Ter. alt:** *Can be* 1500 *ft.* **Downhill run:** *900 ft.* **Time to main summit:** $\frac{1}{2}$ *h.* **Cat:** *1.* **Map:** *No. 68.*

Approach
Take the road to Wanlockhead and Leadhills, accessible from the main Glasgow-Carlisle road at Abington or Elvanfoot or from the Dumfries-Kilmarnock road at Mennock.

At Wanlockhead (1530 ft.) a motor road ascends to the summit of Lowther hill (2378 ft.) where there is a radar station.

Ascent Route
Green Lowther lies a mile to north-east along a broad ridge with a gentle col.

Descent Route
The west side of the hill has numerous gullies leading down towards Wanlockhead, the length of descent depending on the snow line.

Variations
The variations possible are considerable. For medium skiers the descent by the east side of the Riccart Cleuch gives a long run of $2\frac{1}{2}$ miles finishing at 1000 ft. on the top side of the Dalveen pass (A702). Cat: 3.

If the snow line is at 500 ft., a descent from Lowther hill to the south-east takes one down very steep slopes to the Dinabid Linn to Dalveen farm, on the lower end of the pass (700 ft.). Cat: 4.

7 Campsie Fells
1896 ft.

Character: *These are featureless grass hills with steep escarpments that provide an excellent basis for learning off-piste skiing.* **Season:** *December to February. Very little snow cover needed. Does not withstand prolonged thaw.* **Aspect:** *Variable.* **Access:** *Car — excellent. Glasgow, 12 miles.* **Dep. alt:** *1000 ft.* **Ascent:** *Up to 1500 ft., depending on hill chosen.* **Max. downhill run:** *1600 ft.* **Cat:** *1.* **Map:** *No. 60.*

Approach
One high road (Crow Road, B822, Lennoxtown/Fintry) cleaves the Campsie Fells in two, and rises to 1092 ft. The best take off to the fells lies a little south of the highest point. If there is snow, kerbside parking will be at a premium, and there is none other.

Routes
One can ski either to west or east.
East: A popular ascent is Lecket hill (1792 ft.) a mile and half to the east, and visible all the way from the road. A descent and a climb further east brings one to Meikle Bin, a shapely little grass hill above the Carron forest, from which it may also be reached.
West: Immediately west of the road is Holehead (1805 ft.), the eastern end of an undulating plateau of peaks running westwards for four miles to Earls Seat (1896 ft.), the highest of the Fells. If the snow cover is low a spur giving skiing of interest runs west to Drumgoyne hill (1402 ft.). Reach the Strathblane valley at the distillery by the north side of Drumgoyne.

Alternative
The B818 road (Denny to Fintry) also runs through the northern Campsies, through a high valley in which lies the Carron reservoir and forest. Forest roads lead to the upper

43

fells, like Meikle Bin. There are access roads running south-wards from each end of the reservoir. They are marked by a Forestry Commission sign ''Carron Water''.

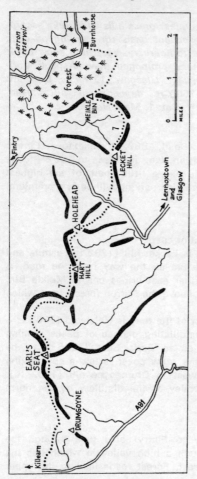

8 Ben Lomond
3192 ft.

Character: *Not only does this peak enjoy one of the finest situations in Scotland but its southern slopes provide a superb ski field.* **Season:** *Due to the southern exposure the season is short — January to early March.* **Aspect:** *South.* **Access:** *Bus — none. Car, good, but at low level. Glasgow, 25 miles.* **Dep. alt:** *80 ft. (see alternative below).* **Ascent:** *3110 ft.* **Ter. alt:** *500 ft.* **Downhill run:** *2600 ft.* **Time to main summit:** *2½ h.* **Cat:** *3.* **Map:** *No. 53.*

Approach
Take the road on the east side of Loch Lomond, accessible from Drymen; follow it to the limit, just past Rowardennan Hotel. The path of Ben Lomond strikes uphill some 400 yds. beyond the parking place in the trees.

Ascent Route
Save in exceptional seasons, Loch Lomondside will be snow free, and skis will have to be carried up the footpath through the forest. Snow normally lies around 500 ft. upward. The rising moorland of grass ahead contains many parallel watercourses, which fill easily with snow, and will provide a skiable route even after prolonged thaw. (The potential of the snowfield can be judged by viewing the mountain from the Stockiemuir road out of Glasgow to Drymen). The final cone of the mountain is steep, and is in places often scoured clear of snow by the wind. If the upper slopes are very barren it is not worth taking skis above about 2900 ft., but more often than not, one may ski to the summit.

Descent Route
The upper 400 ft. of the mountain is steep on all sides, but falls precipitously to the north, and there may be cornices. Keep well to the south and west flanks. Below 2700 ft. the descent is easy and offers opportunities for fast running on

a wide snowfield at an easy angle. It is rare that one can ski down to the car.

Alternative Ascent Route
On the east flank of Ben Lomond is Loch Ard forest, the property of the Lower Clyde Water Board, and forested by the Forestry Commission. It is one of the most beautiful forest regions in Scotland, especially in winter. If permission can be gained to drive from Kinloch Ard to Corriegrennan farm, there is a forest road that rises to over 1000 ft. and takes one within two miles of the summit, on the south side.

9   Doune Hill
2409 ft.   Dunbartonshire

Character: *Grass hills of considerable character and steepness in a fine location. A traverse route involving alternate ascent and descent.* **Season:** *Periodic January to March. Does not withstand prolonged thaw. Must have snow above 750 ft.* **Aspect:** *North and south.* **Access:** *Bus — poor (3 miles). Car, excellent. Luss.* **Dep. alt:** 400 *ft.* **Ascent:** 3850 *ft. total.* **Ter. alt:** 400 *ft.* **Downhill run:** 3750 *ft. total.* **Time to main summit:** 3½–4 *h.* **Cat:** 5. **Map:** 53.

Approach
Follow the A82 (Glasgow to Fort William) road to Luss, which may also be reached by bus. Turn west up Glen Luss to the point where the road crosses the Mallochan burn, just short of Edintaggert farm (3 miles — 400 ft.).

Traverse
First Ascent: 1700 ft. Ascend the steep grass hillside to Mid-Hill (2100 ft.). Skinning quite feasible in spite of angle.

First Descent: 1350 ft. From the south summit of Mid-Hill follow the west spur. This has a steep corrie to the north, which is best avoided till lower down. Reach the col between Mid-Hill and Doune Hill (750 ft.), which is also head of Glen Mallochan.

Second Ascent: 1650 ft. Ascend westwards to summit of Doune Hill (2409 ft.) — a superb viewpoint. The easiest return route now is to continue.

Second Descent: 500 ft. The objective is Beinn Eich. Follow broad slopes at first southwards, and then as the ridge swings S.E. turn S.E. It is well to keep off the crest of the hill, and hold to the Glen Mallochan flank where the snow build up is best, and smoothes out the peat hags.

Third Ascent: 500 ft. Do not attempt to by-pass Beinn Eich by trying a traverse to Edintaggert farm unless you are a skier of the highest calibre and have studied the snow conditions, and are satisfied they are neither too hard nor prone to avalanche. Reach summit of Beinn Eich.

Third and Last Descent: 1900 ft. The south flank of Beinn Eich is the least steep, and is the one to use. There are some very steep sections, and due to the southern exposure and grassy under-surface, they avalanche easily. Treat all steep sections with care. The skiing can be exciting, demanding and delightful.

10 Ben Cleuch
2363 ft.
Clackmannan

Character: *The principal summit in a range of grass hills dominating the Forth valley. Gentle skiing.* **Season:** *Whenever snow is lying at a depth of 10 cm. above 1000 ft.* **Aspect:** *South.* **Access:** *Bus — good. Car — excellent. Dollar.* **Dep. alt:** 750 ft. **Ascent:** 1850 ft. **Ter. alt:** 750 ft. **Downhill run:** 1850 ft. **Time to main summit:** 2½ h. **Cat:** 1. **Map:** *No.* 55.

Approach

Take the steep road at Castle Campbell from Dollar main street (1 mile). It leads to a car park (750 ft.), from which a path leads down to Castle Campbell.

Ascent Route

Ben Cleuch lies roughly in the direction of the river falling into the glen behind Castle Campbell, called the Burn of Sorrow. This is a deeply cut glen and tedious to negotiate but can be avoided. From the car park go through the gate and ascend the shallow glen to the north, reaching the summit of Whitewisp Hill (2110 ft.). This hill and glen form a natural snow bowl. From Whitewisp Hill follow the crest, or if that is blown clear of snow a line somewhat below the crest, due west to Tarmangie Hill (2117 ft.). The view southward is stupendous. Ben Cleuch now lies due west some two and half miles off. Descend the gentle slope to the col with Ben Cleuch (Maddy Moss on O.S. map). The walkers path from Tillicoultry to Glen Devon passes over this col. Ascend the east shoulder to the summit.

Descent Route

For the fastest route, regain Tarmangie Hill and then make a contoured descent to the car park. There is, however, a great deal of skiable snow around Ben Cleuch. A descent may be made on the north side for a while followed by re-ascent to Maddy Moss. The south-west side holds snow very well, and if there is exceptional cover, one can ski right down to Tillicoultry, but this is not in Cat: 1. The best and easiest return to the car is to regain Whitewisp hill, and follow the route of ascent.

Traverse

If there is snow lying down to 750 ft. it is well worth traversing northwards from the summit or Tarmangie hill. This leads down into Glen Devon, held by the Kinross and Fife water board. There is a good road right up to Backhill

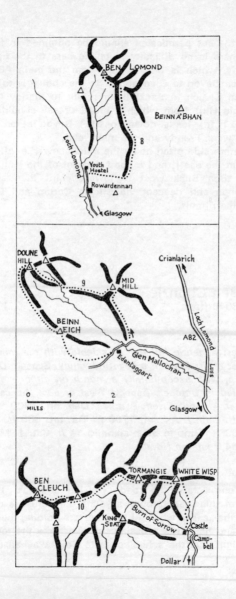

D

(1050 ft.), but permission should be obtained to take cars there. There is no difficulty in taking cars to the dam itself at Frandy, which is only a mile from the main A823 road from Glen Devon to Gleneagles. So the choice is to descend from Ben Cleuch to Backhill, or return to Maddy Moss (or Tarmangie Hill) from which a broad grassy shoulder (Scad Hill, 1921 ft.) leads down to Glen Devon at any chosen point between Frandy and the main road.

The western side often holds the most snow (i.e. after snow-falls from the east), and a good descent of the langlauf type is from Ben Buck west to lowest point then ascent to Blairdennon and descent via Mickle Corum and Glen Tye Hill to Sherrifmuir.

11   Ben Chonzie
3048 ft.   Perthshire

Character: *A gentle hill that is skiable with the minimum of snow, set at the head of a beautiful valley.* **Season:** *December to March, with exceptionally a month on either side. It has been skied in October.* **Aspect:** *West or east.* **Access:** *Bus — none. Car — good. Crieff, 9 miles.* **Dep. alt:** *1300 ft. (max.) or 800 ft. (min.).* **Ascent:** *1700 ft.* **Ter. alt:** *800 ft.* **Downhill run:** *2200 ft.* **Time to main summit:** *1½ h.* **Cat:** *1.* **Map:** *Start on No. 54, route on No. 48.*

Approach
From Comrie take the road up Glen Lednock. The early portion of this road through a young oak forest is delightful early in the season when all the trees are holding their leaves. A mile and half after crossing the river take the rough road to the right past the schoolhouse to Coishavachan (800 ft.),

200 yards beyond under Creag na-h Iolaire. There is a metalled hill track suitable for cars, rather rough, and with only a few turning places. If the snow line is high it is useful to use this road. Permission should be sought at the cottages at Coishavachan. The road rises to a small dam on the Invergeldie burn, and one branch crosses the burn onto the southern flanks of Ben Chonzie (pronounced Ben y Chone), or rather point 2759 ft.

Ascent Route
The gentle grass slopes are scalloped into hollows, and each holds snow well. Make for point 2759 ft. or slightly to its west, gain the ridge and proceed to the summit. The view south over lovely Strathearn is well worthwhile.

Descent Route
Either by route of ascent, or if seeking steeper skiing, directly to the west, crossing the Invergeldie burn, and then skiing down the easy angle of the Invergeldie glen to meet the road.

Variants
On paper the ascent of the peak via Loch Turret looks promising, but the new dam there makes access harder, for the road to the loch head is now a neglected track. However, in conditions of heavy fall, it is interesting to drive to the Loch Turret dam (Glen Turret road, $\frac{1}{2}$ miles west of Crieff) and proceed to ski along the line of the old road to the head of Loch Turret and so up into the corrie to Lochan Caine from which the slopes due west are not too steep and lead to the ridge just south of the summit. On the descent one holds more or less to the long broad ridge running S.E. from point 2579 ft. towards Carn Chois and so back to the dam-head. The road to Loch Turret is in the property of the Mid Scotland water board from whom it may be advisable to seek permission to use the road.

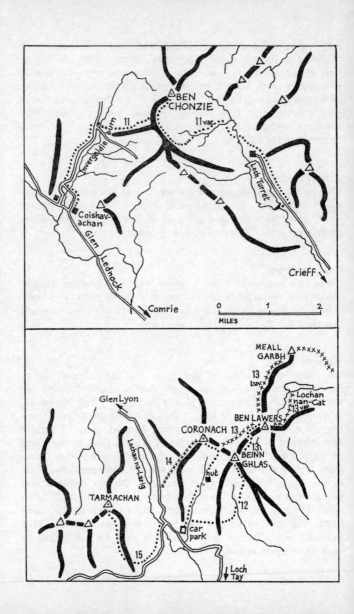

12 Beinn Ghlas
3657 ft.

Character: *A fine accessible peak offering skiing of considerable variety. Very popular skiing area.* **Season:** *The season is much shorter than the height of the mountain would suggest — December to March.* **Aspect:** *South.* **Access:** *Bus — none. Car — excellent. Killin.* **Dep. alt:** *1350 ft.* **Ascent:** 2500 *ft.* **Ter. alt:** 1350 *ft.* **Downhill run:** 2300 *ft.* **Time to main summit:** 2½ *h.* **Cat:** 4. **Map:** *No.* 48.

Approach

A metalled road signposted 'Lochan na Larige' leaves the A827 (Killin to Kenmore) road 4 miles east of Killin, and ascends to a large car park at 1350 ft. It is usually kept clear of snow. Here is National Trust for Scotland information booth and a Scottish Ski Club first aid station. The road continues to the pass (Larig) beyond a dammed loch and descends to Glen Lyon.

The existence of the car park and the easy access to gentle grassy slopes makes this a popular place for skiers of all grades. A gentle grass corrie rises to a col at 3000 ft., below which is a hut belonging to the Scottish Ski Club. There are many runs here.

Ascent Route

From the car park a shallow grassy corrie rises to a col (3000 ft.) between Meall Coronach and Beinn Ghlas. Ascend the track for half a mile, then descend to cross the river at small catchment dam. Ascend shoulder of Beinn Ghlas (path in summer), aiming for the 2000 ft. contour. If there is a paucity of snow, it is often easier to carry skis to the summit along the shoulder, which is usually blown free of snow. Normally, however, continue the contour into the steeper corrie that falls south from the summit of Beinn Ghlas (Coire a' Chonnaidh). It steepens in its upper part and is best left by its east side to gain the N.E. spur of the mountain.

Between this spur and the burn is some of the best skiing on the mountain, largely hidden from the car park. From the spur gain the summit.

Descent Route
As route of ascent. If there is good summit snow cover, and it is possible to ski down the south-east spur, an interesting and steep descent takes one down to the Scottish Ski Club hut.

Variation
The ascent of this peak is often combined with that of Lawers or Coronach.

13 Ben Lawers
3984 ft.   Perthshire

Character: *A superb summit offering a variety of descents.*
Season: *December to March.* **Aspect:** *North-west or North-east.* **Access:** *Bus — none. Car — excellent.* **Dep. alt:** *1350 ft.*
Ascent: *3050 ft.* **Ter. alt:** *1350 ft. (traverse, 850 ft.).*
Downhill run: *2630 ft. (traverse, 3100 ft.).* **Time to main summit:** *3½ h.* **Cat:** 4 *or* 6. **Map:** 48. **Diag:** *R.* 12.

Approach
As for R. 12.

Ascent Route
Ascend Beinn Ghlas by R. 12. From that summit descend along the north ridge to the col with Lawers. The ridge is narrow with small crags, and though cornices are rare here, care should be exercised. Exciting skiing. The inexperienced may wish to walk down. From the col the summit cone of

Lawers lies directly in front. (Alternatively, it is easier to go from Beinn Ghlas to the Lawers col by way of the little east corrie, to a point below the col, to which one must then climb).

Descent Route

If the snow in Coire Chonnaidh looks good, use this descent (R. 12). Otherwise descend by traversing the great N.W. face of the peak to reach the col between Meall Coronach and Beinn Ghlas. Only in spring snow is this descent worthwhile. In mist it is very easy to miss the col and finish up in Glen Lyon.

Traverse

By continuing northwards along the ridge one gains the next peak, Meall Garbh. One can ski off the east ridge of this peak onto the slopes to the north of Lawers burn to finish at Lawernacroy farm, a few minutes walk from the main road at Lawers Hotel.

Variation

The east side of the Lawers summit is formed of steep crags, at the base of which nestles Lochan nan Cat (2350 ft.). By descending 300 ft. down the east ridge, one can find a skiable slope that runs down to the lochan. It is only for the bold and expert skier choosing the right snow conditions. Cat: 6.

14 Meall Coronach
3530 ft.   Perthshire

Character: *A grassy hill that carries snow well, having great character and interest to the skier.* **Season:** *December to*

March, exceptionally one month to each side. **Aspect:** *South-east or South-west.* **Access:** *Bus — none. Car — good.* **Dep. alt:** 1350 *ft.* **Ascent:** 2200 *ft.* **Ter. alt:** 1350 *ft.* **Downhill run:** 2180 *ft.* **Time to main summit:** 2 *h.* **Cat:** 3 *(Lochan na Larig), or Ski Club hut,* 5. **Map:** *No.* 48. **Diag:** *R.* 12.

Approach

See Ben Lawers, R. 12. Note that Meall Coronach is not given as a spot height on the 7th edition of the O.S. map.

Ascent Route

From the car park ascend the corrie to the col at the head of the corrie that runs north from the car park. A narrow ridge ascends steeply to the summit, for which one must carry skis. If one is carrying skis anyway, it is more interesting to walk to the summit via the north spur of the mountain, whose slightly craggy extremity hangs over the car park (Sron Dha Murchdi). Higher up the general exposure of the ridge gives light snow cover and good walking conditions. If skinning all the way to the summit, also follow this ridge, but hold to the east flank, till almost abreast of the Ski Club hut, seen in the corrie below.

Descent Route

A challenging route is to descend direct to the corrie to the S.E. of the summit. After deep fresh falls of snow these slopes can avalanche, category 5. One lands in the upper basin and a run past the hut takes one to the car park.

The classic descent is to run down the S.W. side towards Lochan na Larig. On the upper slopes are fine snowfields, and though lower down there are occasionally ditch-like burns, the running is good, and never steep. If the road is joined too soon, one is faced with poling back to the car. Thus the traverse line picked holds to a point slightly south of the south end of the Dam.

15 Meall nan Tarmachan

3421 ft.

Character: *Varied terrain, steep near the summit.* **Season:** *January to March.* **Aspect:** *East.* **Access:** *Bus — poor. Car — excellent. Killin.* **Dep. alt:** 1600 *ft.* **Ascent:** 1800 *ft.* **Ter. alt:** 1500 *ft.* **Downhill run:** 1900 *ft.* **Time to main summit:** 1¾ *h.* **Cat:** 4 *(1 only, up to 2900 ft.).* **Map:** *No.* 48. **Diag:** *R.* 12.

Approach

As for R. 12. Drive past the car park. Within half a mile a road forks left and crosses the Allt a' Mhoirneas by a road bridge. There is a gate here, sometimes locked. The road is an old hydro board construction road and contours west on the south flanks of the mountain, finally reaching about 2100 ft.

Ascent Route

Leave the hydro road at about 1600 ft. contour (a mile from the bridge) and ski N.W. to ascend and cross the south spur of the peak. Keep to the line of the spur, but hold to its west flank. At 2900 ft. one reaches a small plateau above which the steep final section of the mountain looms. These slopes are dangerous after heavy snowfall, or in conditions where wind slab may have formed.

The ascent from this point is occasionally very steep and calls for side-stepping uphill. The route is impossible to describe, but involves taking snow banks between the small crags and linking them. Work upwards from left to right, that is, in a northerly direction, gaining height wherever possible. One comes out on easier ground about 250 ft. below and to the north of the summit, which is now easily reached.

Descent Route

The descent by the route of ascent is exhilirating, and below 2900 ft. gives fast running in a fine snow bowl.

Traverse and Variation
The northern slopes of the mountain are less crag bound, but almost as steep at one point. They lead down in a straightforward manner to Coire Riadhailt, whose burn meets the north side of the Lochan na Larig road at 1500 ft. This side of the Larig road is not usually kept clear of snow and thus one cannot normally drive to it. But when this is possible it makes a pleasant and easier ascent of the peak, and an excellent traverse.

16 Beinn Dubhchraig
3204 ft.   Perthshire

Character: *A broad easy corrie, offering no difficulty, leading to a peak of interest.* **Season:** *January to March, occasionally later.* **Aspect:** *North-west.* **Access:** *Bus — fair. Car — good. Tyndrum.* **Dep. alt:** *700 ft.* **Ascent:** *2500 ft.* **Ter. alt:** *700 ft.* **Downhill run:** *2500 ft.* **Time to main summit:** *2½ h.* **Cat:** *1.* **Map:** *No. 53.*

Approach
A great deal depends upon one's predeliction for crossing rivers. The skiing is in Coire Dubhchraig on the north side of the mountain. By bus get off where the A82 trunk road crosses the river Fillan 1½ miles south of Tyndrum. Follow the railway line to the point where it crosses the Coninish river. On the left is a stand of old Scots pines (Coille Coire Chuile) which should be gained by crossing a small burn.
By car the above route may also be used, but a quicker route is to take the road to Coninish farm up the glen of the same name. The road turns off about a mile south of Tyndrum. Follow it to the point where it closes on the river. Cross the river here. In spate this is dangerous.

Ascent Route

The ascent is straightforward. The corrie runs south-west. Make for the col immediately to the N.W. of the summit, and then ascend the final 250 ft. to the top.

Descent Route

Follow the route of ascent, and as the corrie is free from danger its whole width may be used.

Variation

If there is good snow cover on the tops, from the col an ascent may be made of Ben Oss (3374 ft.).

Under good spring snow conditions it is pleasant to descend on the south side towards Glen Falloch, reaching the A82 at or about the Falls of Falloch (330 ft.), following the general line of the Fionn Ghleann. One can judge from the summit how far down the snow runs. This route enables one to make some interesting steep skiing down into Loch Oss, a superb high loch nestling under Ben Dubhchraig, and a sun trap.

17 Stuchd an Lochain
3144 ft.
Perthshire

Character: *A fine isolated hill offering very varied terrain.*
Season: *January to March, occasionally a few weeks to each side.* **Aspect:** *North or South-west.* **Access:** *Bus — none. Car good. Fortingal.* **Dep. alt:** *(a) 1350 ft. (b) 1000 ft.* **Ascent:** 1800 ft. or 2140 ft. **Ter. alt:** 1350 ft. or 1000 ft. **Downhill run:** 1800 ft. or 2140 ft. **Time to main summit:** *(a)* 2¼ h. *(b)* 2¾ h. **Cat:** *(a)* 4. *(b)* 3. **Map:** *No. 47.*

Approach

Drive up Glen Lyon, or if coming from the west and the Lochan na Larig road is open cross to the head of Glen Lyon from Killin.

(a)   If permission is granted to use the road, drive to Loch Giorra Lodge (1350 ft.). This road strikes westwards off the Glen Lyon road 1½ miles up the glen from Meggernie Castle. Four miles to the loch from the Glen road.

(b)   Continue up Glen Lyon to Pubil where the Allt Camus-laidh joins the river Lyon.

Ascent Route

(a)   The peak lies directly south. Cross river by the bridge and skirt the shoulder of Creag an Fheadain to reach the corrie of Lochan nan Cat. Do not go to the lochan, but as the corrie eases in angle just below the lochan at about 2200 ft., trend leftwards to reach the col just to the south of point 2909 ft. From the col an ascending traverse to the west leads to the summit.

(b)   From Pubil follow the general line of the Allt Camus-laidh. From about 1750 ft. the peak is visible ahead and any line to the summit can be chosen.

Descent Route

Either of the above routes may be chosen for descent. The middle section of route (b) is shallow in angle and gives poor running unless there is a great deal of consolidated snow. In spring snow it is superb.

Traverse

The peak lends itself to a fine traverse, particularly in spring, starting at Loch Giorra and finishing at Pubil.

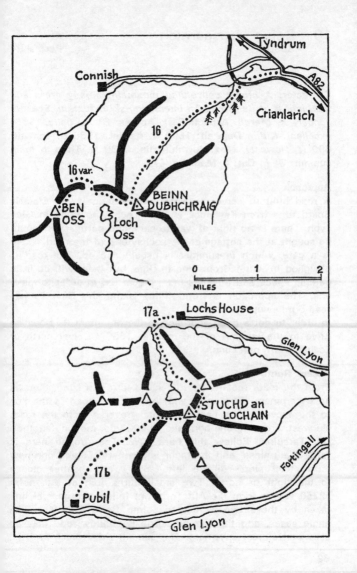

18   Beinn Heasgarnich
3530 ft.

Character: *A highly convoluted mountain, mostly grass and the highest of its group. An interesting ski mountain.* **Season:** *January to March.* **Aspect:** *East.* **Access:** *Bus — none. Car — excellent. Killin.* **Dep. alt:** 1600 *ft.* **Ascent:** 1930 *ft.* **Ter. alt:** 890 *ft. (lowest).* **Max. downhill run:** 2730 *ft.* **Time to main summit:** 2½ *h.* **Cat:** 4. **Map:** *No.* 47.

Approach

A road built to serve the North of Scotland Hydro Electric Board runs from Kenknock in Glen Lochay to Pubil in Glen Lyon. There is no right of way to cars, and permission should be sought at the cottage at the Lochay end of the road. There is a gate, which in summer is usually locked. The road is ploughed in winter from time to time, but there will be little parking space and a shovel must be carried in order to make one. The approach is from Killin, taking the Glen Lochay road 5 miles up the glen.

In order to get a good approach to the mountain it is best to drive to the summit of the road at 1600 ft., just north of Lochan Learg nan Lunn.

Ascent Route

From the road, looking past Lochan Learg nan Lunn, there is an escarpment. The north end, nearest the road is the key to the ascent. On a near horizontal traverse from the road, ski west, crossing one burn and in 400 yds. meeting another, Allt Tarsuinn. Follow this burn S.W. The ground here is fairly featureless, and the moor is heathery. Facing one now is a steep slope to the left (south) and gentler slopes to the right or north. Two small burns join at this point (2250 ft.) to form the Allt Tarsuinn; follow the general line taken by these two as they rise into Coire Ban Mor. The angle eases, and the summit corrie is shallow, and may be ascended almost anywhere. The summit ridge, such as it is, lies north/south, and one will naturally join the ridge south of the summit.

Descent Route
If the snow line is above 1500 ft. it is best to ski back to car by the route of ascent. If it falls below 1500 ft. one can make a direct and steep ascent down to the valley at Badour, 800 ft.

Traverse
The north face of the mountain is steep. N.N.W. from the summit a gentle ridge falls towards Glen Lyon. According to the snow and skill either follow the corrie or the ridge down for a thousand feet, then head towards the junction of the Hydro Board road with Glen Lyon at Pubil.

19   Ben Challum
   3354 ft.   Perthshire

Character: *A fine peak calling for skilful skiing. Needs good snow cover.* **Season:** *February.* **Aspect:** *South-west.* **Access:** *Bus — poor. Car — good. Crianlarich.* **Dep. alt:** *600 ft.* **Ascent:** 2750 *ft.* **Ter. alt:** *600 ft.* **Downhill run:** *2750 ft.* **Time to main summit:** *2¾ h.* **Cat:** *4.* **Map:** *No. 47 (53 useful).*

Approach
Take the farm road to Auchtertyre, which leaves the A82 main road a mile and half south of Tyndrum on the east side of the river Fillan. Obtain permission to park the car at Auchtertyre farmhouse (shown only on Map 53).

Ascent Route
Cross the West Highland railway line (tunnel) and ascend in a N.E. direction directly up the hillside. At about 2000 ft.

arrive on a broad shoulder with many dips and bumps. One is now on sheet 47 of the O.S. map. The mountain rises directly ahead and is fairly steep for the last thousand feet. The south top is not the true summit.

Descent Route
On the descent of the upper mountain it is often best to hold to the west flank, though it pays to regain the flat shoulder at 2200 ft. and then retrace the route of ascent.

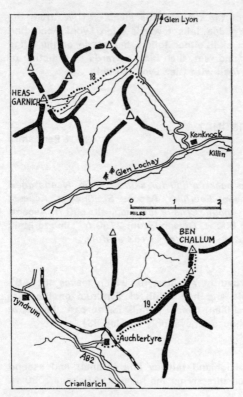

20 Clach Leathad
3602 ft.   Argyllshire
Stob Gabhar
3565 ft.

Character: *Highly varied ridges and corries, often challenging; superb situations.* **Season:** *January to March. Needs good snow cover for Stob Gabhar.* **Aspect:** *North-east.* **Access:** *Bus – good. Car – excellent.* **Dep. alt:** *3550 ft.* **Ascent:** *2560 ft.* **Ter. alt:** *1050 ft.* **Downhill run:** *4600 ft.* **Time to main summit:** *3½ h.* **Cat:** *5.* **Map:** *No. 47.*

Approach
Leave the car at the White Corries car park, off the A82 at the entrance of Glencoe.

Ascent Route – *Clach Leathad*
Take the 'White Corries' lift system to highest point just below the summit of Meall a Bhuiridh, which should be ascended. Clach Leathad lies due west, and is not normally a ski run. Walk down to the col (3000 ft.) and ascend the peak. In hard snow crampons are useful but not essential. Ice-axe advisable.

First Descent Route
This descent is superb. Ski down the broad summit ridge in a south-westerly direction till faced with a wide and very steep slope leading down to a low col, the Bealach Fuar Chataidh that divides Coire Ba from Glen Etive. In mist it would require excellent route finidng to locate the col. The slope is over 1000 ft. high and steep, and may have a number of rocks protruding. Descend with care till satisfied that the snow is suitable for skiing.

Second Ascent Route – *Stob Gabhar*
It is possible to abandon the route here, and ski down into Coire Ba. Note that the south side of Clach Leathad is prone

E

to avalanche, and avoid it. For the ascent first gain the long shoulder of Aonach Mor by an undulating ridge that runs south-west. Once on Aonach Mor turn left (south-east), and follow the ridge to the summit.

Second Descent Route
Regain the Bealach Fuar-Chataidh by route of ascent. The objective now is to reach Ba cottage at the mouth of the corrie. Too steep a line initially will leave one poling across the flat intermediate ground, while too high a line will take one onto the potentially avalanche prone slopes of the south face of Clach Leathad. Take the highest line consistent with safety. If one wishes to end the day on the pistes of Meall a Bhuirdh, climb by the Allt Coire an Easain to reach the shallow spur below the S.E. spur of Meall a Bhuiridh, from which a traverse can be made to the N.E. plateau.
For a direct return to the car park, contour the slopes of Creag an Fhirich to Ba cottage (1159 ft.), a ruin in a superb setting. From here the old military road leads back to the car park on an easy col, but better and faster is to climb the flank of Meall a Bhuiridh in N.N.W. direction to area marked on the map as Leacann nam Braonon. A 45 min. climb takes one to about 1800 ft., from which point a descending traverse leads to the car park.

21   Stob Coire Easain
3545 ft.   Inverness-shire

Character: *One of the finest ski ascents in Scotland amidst scenery of alpine grandeur.* **Season:** *January to April.* **Aspect:** *North.* **Access:** *Car — poor. Bus — none.* **Dep. alt:** *400 ft.* **Ascent:** *3200 ft.* **Ter. alt:** *1100 ft.* **Max. downhill run:** *2400 ft.* **Time to main summit:** *3½ h.* **Cat:** *4.* **Map:** *Nos. 47, 36, or Ben Nevis & Glencoe Tourist edition.*

Approach

(a) From the A82 road take the turning south marked 'Lianachan', 1 mile west of Spean Bridge, leading to the farm of that name. Park here. Continue on foot on a dirt road maintained by the Forestry Commission, which branches 100 yd. further on. Take the left fork 200 yd. down to a

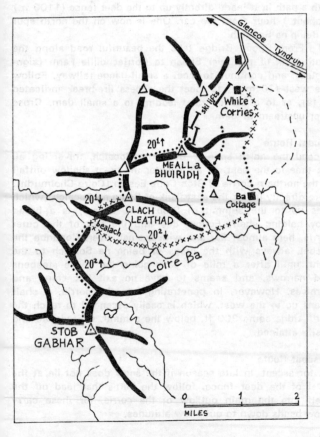

MILES

beautiful river (Allt Coille-rais) with ford and stepping stones. A barely noticeable path runs left (N.E.) through the woods to a bridge in 100 yd. Follow the path into a clearing with a ruined bothy, and take the right hand of the two tracks, which follows a fire-break through the forest.

After a mile turn left at a small gauge railway. Follow it over the next river (Cour) and continue for 400 yd. till a fire-break with a path in it leads directly up to the deer fence (1100 ft.) — about 1 hour from the car. One is now on the north spur of Beinn na Socaich.

(b)   From Spean Bridge take the beautiful road along the south bank of the river Spean to Corriechoillie Farm (sign-posted), and continue to meet a small gauge railway. Follow this west (30 min.) to meet the access fire-break indicated in (a), or to a branch road leading to a small dam. Cross river upstream of dam.

Ascent Route

Ascend the north spur of Beinn na Socaich, traversing all the time to the east, so as to enter the great shallow outfall of the northern corrie of Stob Coire Easain (Coire Choimlidh). Here directly under the east flank of Beinn na Socaich (which runs up to the summit of Stob Coire Easain) is a broad snow-holding shelf. Follow this into the bed of the outer corrie, here almost flat and with a small river. Continue the ascent, always with the crags of Beinn na Socaich to the right, until after a mile of easy going the corrie steepens and narrows, and seems to have no exit but crags and cornices. However, in penetrating into the corrie, a shelf opens up to the west, which is easily ascended to reach the north ridge some 300 ft. below the summit, now visible and easily attained.

Descent Route

As for ascent. In late season if the snow does not lie at the level of the deer fence, follow the burns that lead off the shelf into the main outflow of the corrie, for these carry snow bands down to quite low altitudes.

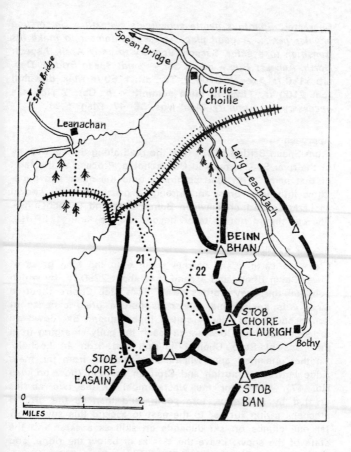

22   Stob Choire Claurigh
3858 ft.

Character: *Spacious gentle snowfields beneath a rim of fine angular peaks. A good place for a mountaineer to make his transition to a skier.* **Season:** *January to early April.* **Aspect:** *North.* **Access:** *Bus — none. Car — good. Spean Bridge.* **Dep. alt:** 1150 *ft.* **Ascent:** 2700 *ft.* **Ter. alt:** 1150 *ft.* **Max. downhill run:** 2100 *ft.* **Time to main summit:** 4 *h.* **Cat:** 2 *(ice axe necessary for summit).* **Map:** *Nos.* 36, 47. **Diag:** *R.*21.

Approach

From Spean Bridge (A82) take the road along the south bank of the river Spean, marked Corriechoille. Proceed to the farm of that name. The road continues onto the moor and penetrates into new forest and through a gap in the hills known as Larig Leachdach between Beinn Bhan and Cruach Innse. The car should not be taken beyond the tree line (1150 ft.).

Ascent Route

From the Larig road cut due south onto the long grass of lower Beinn Bhan, and ascend it to about 2750 ft., by which point all the Grey Corries peaks from Stob Choire Claurigh westwards are visible. Ahead is now a great expanse of gentle snowfields ideally suited to beginners. Ski down on a gentle traversing descent to reach the gully emerging from the base of Stob Choire Claurigh and Sron an Lochain. Another unnamed spur will be seen running from the main ridge between Claurigh and Sron an Lochain (now on map No. 47). Make for the westernmost of the two corries created by this spur, turn south, and then as the ground steepens swing further to the east to ascend this spur. How far one climbs on ski depends on skill as a skier and the state of the snow. Leave the skis at or below the ridge, and ascend the main summit (Claurigh) or Stob Coire Easain (3545 ft.) on foot.

Variations

For a long day when there is plenty of snow one may descend Coire Rath to the south to the col with Stob Ban (3217 ft.), followed by a descent eastwards down the Allt a'Chuil Choirean to the bothy at the end of the Larig road. It is less than 1 h. walk back to the car, and the descent is better than down Beinn Bhan.

23 Ben Nevis
4406 ft.
Inverness-shire

Character: *The only good reason for climbing this magnificent peak is because it is the highest in the British Isles. It is not an ideal skiing mountain due to the long carry on the lower section.* **Season:** *February to May.* **Aspect:** *West.* **Access:** *Bus — poor. Car — poor.* **Dep. alt:** *100 ft.* **Ascent:** *4300 ft.* **Ter. alt:** *100 ft.* **Max. downhill run:** *2000 ft.* **Time to main summit:** *3½ h.* **Cat:** *3.* **Map:** *No. 47, or Ben Nevis tourist edition.*

Approach

From Ft. William drive either to Achintee farm in Glen Nevis, or to the youth hostel on the south bank of the river, and cross to Achintee by footbridge.

Ascent Route

A well made, but now decayed track runs from Achintee up the flank of Meall an-t-Suidhe to a saddle with a lochan at 2300 ft. This is about the lowest point at which skiing is likely to start or finish. The route is simply to follow the cairned track which leads on to the summit plateau at about 3900 ft., and continues to the summit. For the most part the track will be snowed in and invisible, but many cairns will show. The line of ascent keeps to the shoulder south of the Red burn, so named on account of the red coloured rock that shows.

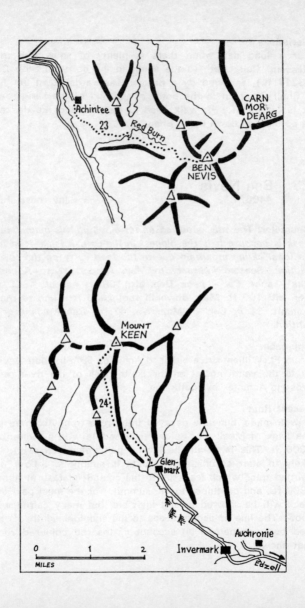

CARN
MOR
DEARG

Achintee

23

Red Burn

BEN
NEVIS

MOUNT
KEEN

24

Glenmark

Auchronie

Invermark

Edzell

0   1   2
MILES

Descent Route
The summit plateau is spacious, but care must be taken to keep well back from the heavily corniced north face. The descent follows the Red burn or its left hand or southern side. At about 3500 ft. it steepens considerably, and the skier must take to the left bank. The burn has a bar of cliffs low down, 200 ft. above the lochan.

24 Mount Keen
3077 ft.

Character: *A gentle hill with steep flanks set at the head of an exquisite glen.* **Season:** *December to March.* **Aspect:** *South.* **Access:** *Car – good, Bus – none. Brechin.* **Dep. alt:** *900 ft. (or 1050 ft.).* **Ascent:** 2177 ft. **Ter. alt:** *900 ft. (or 1050 ft.).* **Downhill run:** 2177 ft. **Time to main summit:** *Glen Mark,* 1½ *h. Invermark,* 2½ *h.* **Cat:** *1 (direct descent, 5).* **Map:** *No. 42.*

Approach
Drive up Glen Esk from Edzell to the end of the public road just short of Invermark Lodge. A good road continues up the west side of Glen Mark, but is private. Entrance at Invermark Lodge, whose entrance gates stand at the end of the public road. If permission is granted a short drive takes one to Glen Mark cottage (1050 ft.). If not, take the car along the Mounth track to Ballater (signposted) for half a mile, and park at the deer fence. The walk to Glen Mark is under an hour and delightful. If snow is below 900 ft. this approach is best.

Ascent Route

The Mounth track is now fit for four-wheel drive vehicles, and provides an obvious route of ascent that is graded and most suitable for skins. Moreover the existence of this road almost to the summit of Mount Keen provides a snow ribbon all the way up the mountain almost irrespective of general snow conditions. The track disappears in winter into the large southern snowfields of the mountain. The summit is well defined.

Descent Route

The descent of the upper slopes is a matter of preference. They are wide and easy. The final descent to Glen Mark cottage on the line of the road is not graded, and beginners may have trouble here, or have to kick turn.

For more expert skiers the most exciting descent is to avoid following the road down into Ladders burn, and to climb slightly onto the top of Couternach, the rocky promontory immediately above Glen Mark. Its west flank catches the snow, and though there is a 50 ft. section that is very steep and narrow, the flank as a whole makes a good steep ski descent.

Variation

It is easy to link Braid Cairn (2907 ft.) to Mt. Keen, and then ski down its southern flank. By holding to the plateau promontory between Eastern burn and Ladders burn, one comes out directly above the lower defile of Ladders burn. Here are several well filled gullies providing good snow tongues by which the valley may be reached. Cat: 4.

25 Boustie Ley
2868 ft.

Character: *A ski round of great charm amongst grassy hills and deep corries. Steep in places.* **Season:** *January to early April.* **Aspect:** *East.* **Access:** *Bus and Car — excellent.* **Dep. alt:** *750 ft.* **Ascent:** *2450 ft.* **Ter. alt:** *800 ft.* **Downhill run:** *2490 ft.* **Time to main summit:** *2½ h.* **Cat:** *4.* **Map:** *Nos. 42 or 41.*

Approach
From the B953, Clova to Kirriemuir road, ascend by the slopes behind Clova Hotel.

Ascent Route
From the Clova Hotel make up the hillside for Loch Brandy. From there it is possible to ascend the Snub, between Loch Brandy and Coire of Clova, but the easiest and recommended route is to head for Green Hill (2837 ft.). From the summit ski round the head of the Corrie to the main summit.

Descent Route
One may, if enthusiastic about steep snow, ski down the Corrie of Clova to the hotel. The present route calls for skiing N.W. across the plateau till beyond Carn Dearg (2695 ft.), and gaining the valley by the western slopes of this hill. These lead back to camping ground just short of the Glen Doll youth hostel.

Variation
In spring, when the snow may have gone from the lower slopes, the burn running from Greenhill down to Inchdowrie House holds the snow well, and makes for a convenient means of access and descent, provided one can master tight turns in narrow ribbons of snow. To the east lies Loch Wirral, and another two snow-holding burns. It is a simple matter to judge at the time which provides the best descent.

If as sometimes happens, the best snow lies on the S.W. slopes of Ben Tirran, then after ascending Green Hill, turn east, contour round the head of the Craigs of Loch Wirral, and reach Ben Tirran (2939 ft.), from which a broad snow-field leads into a burn running to the Glen Clova road.

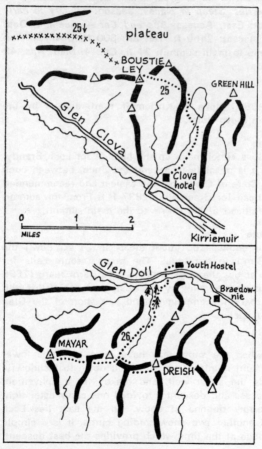

26 Driesh
3105 ft.
Angus
Mayar
3043 ft.

Character: *Everything from narrow trails and steep slopes to broad plateaus.* **Season:** *January to March.* **Aspect:** *North.* **Access:** *Bus — good but very infrequent service. Car — good.* **Dep. alt:** *800 ft.* **Ascent:** *2300 ft.* **Ter. alt:** *800 ft.* **Downhill run:** *2300 ft.* **Time to main summit:** *3 h.* **Cat:** *Various, according to routes taken. Easiest, 4.* **Map:** *41, though 42 shows most of route.*

Approach
Drive to head of Glen Clova, as near as permitted to Glen Doll Youth Hostel.

Ascent Route
Take the Glen Doll path from the youth hostel, and within 100 yd. look for the bridge crossing the White Water. Follow the forest path up the glen on the south side of the White Water for less than a mile when a turning uphill clearly leads up into the north corrie of Driesh, out of which flows the Kilbo burn. The forest finishes at about 1600 ft. and shortly after there is a deer fence. Continue up the corrie, gaining height on the right (north) flank known as the Shank of Drumfollow. The objective is the col at the head of the corrie (it is in fact hardly a col at all, but appears as such). The final 500 ft. are steep, and care should be taken if there is deep fresh snow or wind slab. The easiest line is to reach the col by a traverse in from the right. From the col, Mayar (3043 ft.) lies due west 1½ miles, and Driesh due east 1 mile.

Descent Route
The simplest route (Cat: 4) is the route of ascent. If the snow is good an exciting descent is to ski directly N.W. from

the summit of Driesh. Though the map shows no crags, in fact there are many. Only in one region can one penetrate a short band of crags, broached by a gully, after which wide but steep slopes lead to the floor of the corrie (Cat: 5).

Traverse
If there is deep snow down it is possible to leave Driesh by the east, reaching a col between it and Hill of Strone (2778 ft.). From here steep snow leads into the corrie to the south of the Winter Corrie of Driesh. The last 500 ft. are heathery and need very good cover to be any good. There is a bridge on the Clova river convenient to this route, half a mile south of Braedownie farm.

27 Lochnagar (Clova)
3786 ft.
Aberdeenshire

Character: *A superb mountain approached by a high level undulating plateau that gives one of the finest ski tours in Scotland; long but rarely steep.* **Season:** *February to April.* **Aspect:** *South.* **Access:** *The limit of approach by bus or car is Glen Doll Youth Hostel. Bus service infrequent (Kirriemuir).* **Dep. alt:** *800 ft.* **Ascent:** *3800 ft.* **Ter. alt:** *800 ft.* **Downhill run:** *3800 ft.* **Time to main summit:** *5 h.* **Cat:** *4, skins essential.* **Map:** *No. 41.*

Approach
Drive to the head of Glen Clova, as near as permitted to Glen Doll Youth Hostel.

Ascent Route

There are many occasions when skis may be put on in the
Glen Doll Youth Hostel grounds, and in early season the
route will not be attempted if this is not so. In late season
the major part of the route, which is high level, is so good,
that a walk of two miles up Glen Doll is not a serious de-
traction.

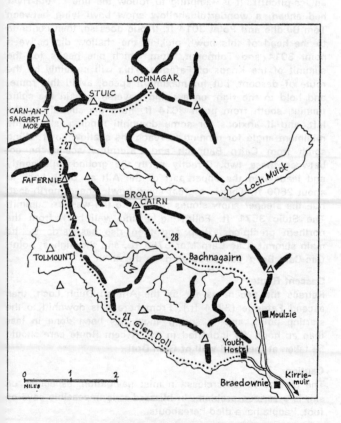

Follow the forestry road up Glen Doll. It peters into a path as the head wall is approached, which climbs up the steep southern flank of Cairn Damff. This path is usually obliterated by snow. The path, known as 'Jock's Road' is a well travelled route to Braemar via Glen Callater. After the steep section one enters a shallow gully (which on the descent can in mist misleadingly take one directly down to Glen Doll via an ice-pitch!!). It is tempting to follow the line of the river bed ahead, a wonderful shallow snow bowl lying between Tom Buidhe and Point 3014 ft. If one does so, then continue to the head of this bowl, picking the shallow dip between point 3014 and Tolmount, from which one heads for the summit of the Knaps of Fafernie. This will certainly be the route of descent, but for maximum speed, avoid this route, and hold to the right on a rising traverse to gain the spine running south from point 3014 ft. Pass the summit on the left, and if anxious for some downhill running, ski at the minimum angle for running to reach the shallow bowl falling south from Cairn Bannoch and Fafernie. Ascend the col between these two. Directly north the ground falls gently and leads into the upper part of the Allt an Dubh Loch at about 2800 ft. This is a great snow bowl. Ahead, north-east, rise the steeper snow slopes running to the western summit, The Stuic 3571 ft. Following a line well back from the northern precipices; drop and then rise eastwards to the main summit, Cac Carn Mor 3768 ft., and the highest point, Cac Carn Beag, some 150 yards to the north.

Descent Route

Retrace the ascent as far as the Allt an Dubh Loch, then ascend Fafernie (3274 ft.). From here it is downhill to the starting point, and in spring snow has been done in less than an hour. As indicated in the Ascent Route care should be taken at the head wall of Glen Doll.

Caution

The plateau is featureless. In mist navigation, especially on ski, is a serious problem. In blizzard it is impossible save on foot. People have died hereabouts.

Traverse

In good snow conditions the traverse onwards down the north side is most rewarding. Whether coming from the Stuic, as some prefer, over the summit of Carn an t-Saigart Mor (3430 ft.), follow the Allt a Coire Duibh leading down into Ballochbuie forest. At the point where the burn enters the forest pick up the path, which becomes better and wider as the descent continues. Lower down the variety of forest roads is confusing, and one is advised always to trend left-wards but downwards. If the correct route is taken, emerge at Invercauld bridge (house) and the main Braemar-Aberdeen road. Braemar 3 miles.

28 Broad Cairn
3268 ft.

Angus/Aberdeenshire

Character: *An uncomplicated mountain set in a magnificent snow-holding area.* **Season:** *February to April.* **Aspect:** *South and South-east.* **Access:** *Bus — poor. Car — good. Kirriemuir.* **Dep. alt:** *900 ft.* **Ascent:** *2400 ft.* **Ter. alt:** *900 ft.* **Downhill run:** *2400 ft.* **Time to main summit:** *3 h.* **Cat:** *3.* **Map:** *No. 41.* **Diag:** *R. 27.*

Approach

Drive to the head of Glen Clova, from Kirriemuir. It is advisable, if permission is obtained, to continue up Glen Clova to the furthest point of the road at Moulzie cottage.

Ascent Route

From Moulzie, follow the track up the glen, (footbridge a mile from Moulzie), to reach Bachnagairn, a ruined bothy in a fine stand of larches (excellent camping). One would

81

F

expect to put on skis here even in late season. Follow the burn (Burn of Gowal) to reach a flat area beneath the Craig of Gowal. The burn continues uphill in a N.N.W. direction, forming, in winter, a superb snow basin, out of which one strikes to gain the summit of Broad Cairn on the right.

Descent Route
As for route of ascent, though if wind is light and snow cover is good, one may without re-ascent come past the top of Craig of Gowal to reach an even finer snow bowl falling from Fafernie and Carn Bannoch.

29 Glas Maol
3502 ft.   Angus

Character: *A fine isolated peak, very accessible to the mechanised facilities, offering exceptionally easy skiing.* **Season:** *December to April.* **Aspect:** *West.* **Access:** *Car — excellent.* **Dep. alt:** *2900 ft.* **Ascent:** *600 ft.* **Ter. alt:** *1700 ft.* **Downhill run:** *1800 ft.* **Time to main summit:** *¾ h.* **Cat:** *1, when not icy. Direct route,* 5. **Map:** *No. 41.*

Approach
Drive to the car park below the Scottish Ski Club hut on the Aberdeenshire side of the Cairnwell Pass (2199 ft.).

Ascent Route
Take the drag lift on the east side and continue skiing eastwards for a third of a mile to gain the Dundee Ski Club, Meall Odhar tow, which take. Glas Maol lies directly ahead. Beginners are warned that the last 200 ft. are not easy if it is icy, and that a slip under these circumstances can be serious.
After the steep section, a gentle walk leads onto the summit.

Descent Route

The objective is to reach the Cairnwell-Braemar road some 2 miles north of the Cairnwell. Old fence posts show the march between Aberdeenshire and Angus. Follow these northwards on broad easy snow slopes with infinite room to manoeuvre. After about a mile a shoulder runs N.W., Sron na Gaoithe. Follow it, holding to the S.W. side, to get best snow and so reach the road at about 1700 ft.

A disadvantage of this route is the need to cross a river at the foot, but it is small, and generally a simple matter.

Variations

The ascent of Glas Maol can be followed by a descent to the head of Glen Isla, or with an ascent of Tolmount (see R.23 and 20) via Carn na Claise. If this is not done as a traverse, the descent on the return down Sron na Gaoithe is still recommended.

Direct Descent

The direct descent of the mountain by the route of ascent calls for skilful skiing for 2–300 ft., and if icy is Cat: 5.

30 Carn an Tuirc
3340 ft.   Aberdeenshire

Character: *A most accessible hill, affording skiing of far greater interest than would appear from the road, and leading to immense gentle snowfields beyond.* **Season.** *January to mid-April.* **Aspect:** *West.* **Access:** *Bus — none. Car — good.* **Dep. alt:** *1700 ft.* **Ascent:** *1650 ft.* **Ter. alt:** *1700 ft.* **Downhill run:** *1650 ft.* **Time to main summit:** *1¾ h.* **Cat:** *3.* **Map:** *No. 41.* **Diag:** *R. 29.*

Approach

The A93 Perth to Braemar road is taken to a point 1½ miles below the summit of the Cairnwell Pass on the north side, about half a mile above the point where the main road crosses the river Cluanie. Lay-by.

Ascent Route

Below the lay-by is an old stone bridge dating back to the original Cairnwell Pass road. Use this to gain the vestigial path up the north bank of the Allt a Garbh Choire. If, however, there is skiable snow at 1700 ft. use the south bank which holds snow much better. 20 min. easy walking leads to the base of the mountain, and any line leading to the apparent summit will suffice. It is best to end the ascent on the south shoulder. The summit is very rocky and as a rule unskiable.

Descent Route

The west face, seen from the road, has large snow wreaths at all times in the winter and is the fastest route of descent. Longer and more interesting is to ski to the east to the col with Carn na Claise, then work down the south facing corrie that leads back to the Allt a Garbh Choire.

Variation

To the east of the mountain are vast gentle slopes that hold snow extremely well. Carn na Claise (3484 ft.) is less than an hour's run, and offers a superb variety of descents, from the extremely steep headwall of the Garbh Choire to the circuit that runs round to Sron na Gaoithe just above the starting point. If doing this be sure to hold to the north side of the Sron na Gaoithe spur to take advantage of the excellent snow that clings to its final nose, just above the car parking place. For route finding it is useful to note that the county march between Aberdeenshire and Angus is very obvious as a line of stakes, and that once having gained Carn na Claise, the stakes run all the way south to Glas Maol or east to Tolmount, thus affording considerable navigational security in doubtful conditions.

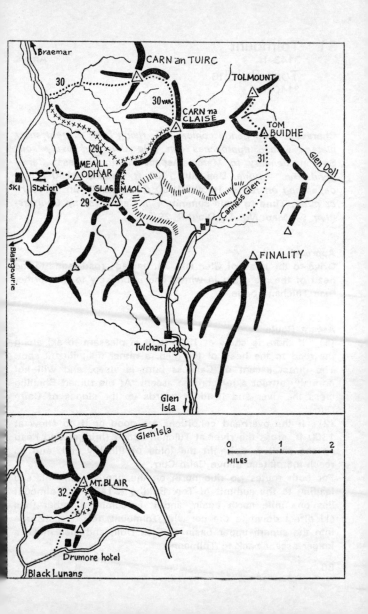

Braemar

CARN an TUIRC

30

30 var.

CARN na
CLAISE

TOLMOUNT

TOM
BUIDHE

29

MEAILL
ODHAR

SKI

Station

GLAS MAOL

29

Glen Doll

31

Canness Glen

Blairgowrie

FINALITY

Tulchan Lodge

Glen
Isla

0   1   2

MILES

Glen Isla

MT. BLAIR

32

Drumore hotel

Black Lunans

31 Tolmount
3143 ft.

Tom Buidhe
3140 ft.

Character: *Two gentle conical hills rising from a great snow plateau whose approaches can give skiing of every sort.* **Season:** *January to March.* **Aspect:** *South.* **Access:** *Car — good. Bus — none.* **Dep. alt:** *1300 ft.* **Ascent:** *2150 ft., or depending on route.* **Ter.alt:** *1300 ft.* **Downhill run:** *2150 ft. or more.* **Time to main summit:** *4 h.* **Cat:** *3 (or by Cannessglen, 5).* **Map:** *No. 41.* **Diag:** *R. 29.*

Approach
Drive to the head of Glen Isla. An unmade road leads to the head of the glen, but in winter one is unlikely to get further than Tulchan Lodge.

Ascent Route
(1) If there is snow at 1300 ft. it is pleasant to ski along the road to the head of the glen, a rather magnificent spot. The direct ascent of Canness burn is steep, and will not normally attract skiers on the ascent. At the ruined Sheiling cross the river and head eastwards up the slopes of Cairn Curr.

(2) If the overhead conditions are good or if no snow at 1300 ft. cross the river at Tulchan Lodge (bridge) and head up the shallow coire in the folds of Finality Hill, and so reach the plateau above Cairn Curr.

For both routes go due north on the gently rising plateau leading to the summit of Tom Buidhe (3140 ft.). Tolmount lies one mile north again, and it is common, rather than ski direct down to the col with Tolmount, to ski eastwards into the superb upper basin of Glen Doll, and then make a longer ascent back to Tolmount.

Descent Route

By leaving Tolmount in a S.W. direction, it is possible to regain the valley without climbing, but with a little poling during a flat section. From the flat section turn south; this route, however, brings one to the cliffed edge of Canness Glen.

Care must be exercised here. For Cat: 5 skiers, work round to the eastern side of the corrie, and then descend the steep slopes to the glen-foot. For Cat: 3 skiers, return by the route of ascent, skirting Tom Buidhe to cut climbing to the minimum.

Traverse

It is common to include either of the two summits in a traverse between any of the following glens :—
Glens Callater, Clova, Isla and the Cairnwell Pass.

32   Mount Blair
2441 ft.   Angus

Character: *A prominent conical hill well seen from lower lower Glenshee, offering very accessible skiing.* **Season:** *January to February.* **Aspect:** *South.* **Access:** *Bus — none. Car — good. Blairgowrie.* **Dep. alt:** *1000 ft.* **Ascent:** *1440 ft.* **Ter. alt:** *1000 ft.* **Downhill run:** *1440 ft.* **Time to main summit:** *2¼ h.* **Cat:** *3.* **Map:** *No. 49.*

Approach

From the Glenshee main road (A93) take the Blacklunans road and go on to Drumore Hotel.
(Ski-lift for beginners).

Ascent Route

Ascend the fields to the north, cross a spur and enter a shallow valley. The summit is directly above. The best slopes lie on the west side.

Descent Route

Follow the route of ascent, though for good skiers it is more interesting to descend by the S.E. spur, and then dip into the head of the shallow valley mentioned above.

Traverse

A good snow collection area lies on the north side, and is better used on the ascent than descent. To reach it do not turn left at Blacklunans, but continue up the riverside for three miles, then turn right for Glen Isla. Halt at highest point, 1187 ft.

33 Glas Tulachan
3445 ft.
Perthshire

Character: *A fine hill with long corries.* **Season:** *January to March.* **Aspect:** *South.* **Access:** *Bus — poor. Car — good. Blairgowrie.* **Dep. alt:** *1250 ft.* **Ascent:** *2200 ft.* **Ter. alt:** *1250 ft.* **Downhill run:** *2200 ft.* **Time to main summit:** *3 h.* **Cat:** 3. **Map:** *No. 41.*

Approach

From the Spittal of Glenshee take the road marked "Dalmunzie House Hotel", and drive to it.

Ascent Route

From the hotel follow the westward glen, Glen Lochsie, as far as the lodge (2½ miles). There is an old railway line here. From the lodge, strike north into a gentle corrie that leads to the summit.

Descent Route
From this summit one can pick off three very fine adjacent summits: Beinn Iutharn Mohr and Bheag and Mam nan Carn.

Traverse
Fealar Lodge, the highest inhabited house in Scotland (1750 ft.), has a reputation for greeting winter visitors, for it is cut off for months at a time. From Glas Tulachan ski west (steep) into Gleann Mor and so reach the access road from Kirkmichael to Fealar. From Beinn Iutharn Mor, Fealar lies only a short skiing time due west.

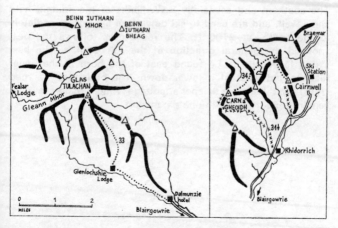

34   Carn a'Gheoidh

3194 ft.   Perthshire

Character: *Never steep, but always interesting skiing.* **Season:** *January to March.* **Aspect:** *South-east.* **Access:** *Excellent. Braemar or Blairgowrie.* **Dep. alt:** *2900 ft.* **Ascent:** *800 ft.* **Ter. alt:** 1300 *ft.* **Downhill run:** *2400 ft.* **Time to main summit:** 1¼ *h.* **Cat:** 4. **Map:** *No.* 41.

Approach
Take the A93 Perth to Braemar road to the Cairnwell Pass and take the Cairnwell chairlift to the top station.

Ascent Route
From the top station ski down the N.W. shoulder of the Cairnwell (normally a piste for ¾ mile) to Loch Vrotachan. Carn a'Gheoidh is now two miles distant in a W.S.W. direction, and is reached by an ascending traverse.

Descent Route
The southern and especially S.W. flanks of the summit hold snow well, and are used to ski down to a flat col immediately to the south, at 2700 ft. The route now follows the best snow in the general direction of the Allt Coolah. The best skiing is usually to be found east of the burn in the upper reaches and west of it lower down. The burn hits the road (A93) just below a keeper's cottage which makes a convenient rendezvous with one's transport.

35 Schichallion
3547 ft.

Character: *A high narrow mountain with steep flanks giving airy but straightforward skiing.* **Season:** *February to March.* **Aspect:** *East and North-east.* **Access:** *Bus — none. Car — good. Kenmore.* **Dep. alt:** *1078 ft.* **Ascent:** *2500 ft.* **Ter. alt:** *1078 ft.* **Downhill run:** *2400 ft.* **Time to main summit:** *2¼ h.* **Cat:** 3. **Map:** *No. 48.*

Approach
Take the B846 from Coshieville (Kenmore 2 miles) or the south Tummel road from Pitlochry to the point where they meet at Tomphubil House in a small plantation. Here a road forks west over the moor under the north face of the mountain. Go to Braes of Foss farm (2½ miles).

Ascent Route
On the upper side of the road from Braes of Foss farm is a small larch plantation with a burn running to its east. Walk through the field east of the burn. The gate at the top end leads to a track (not shown on map). One branch heads through the Bealach towards Gleann Mor to the south. Take a branch that runs into the shallow corrie under the eastern end of the mountain, and reach the summit ridge at around 2250 ft. From here the route follows the crest.

Descent Route
Though the summit ridge collects snow well, especially on its north and south flanks, there are several rocky crowns which break the continuous snow cover. The easiest and finest line of descent is to hold to the southern edge, where the ridge is scalloped into shallow bowls, between the rocky crowns, and except in a poor season, link together. On reaching the eastern end of the ridge at about 2250 ft. drop down by the line of ascent.

Variation
This mountain does not hold snow on its summit ridge over long periods of thaw. However, the north face does. There are several points at which one can dip into the north face. Just east of the summit a steep fan shaped corrie provides a challenging descent (Cat: 5), which should be avoided if the snow is icy. Such a descent would take one to the road about 2 miles west of the farm. However, a less demanding route is to keep to the summit ridge till about 3000 ft., and then look for a way down the north side back to the corrie of the ascent. Pick the line during the ascent. Cat: 4.

36   Beinn a Chuallaich
2925 ft.   Perthshire

Character: *An accessible ski hill offering modest skiing, but a fabulous view of the skiing hills of the Central Highlands.*
Season: *January to March.* **Aspect:** *South-east.* **Access:** *Bus — none. Car — good. Kinloch Rannoch.* **Dep. alt:** *950 ft.* **Ascent:** *2000 ft.* **Ter. alt:** *950 ft.* **Downhill run:** *1800 ft.* **Time to main summit:** *1½ h.* **Cat:** *2.* **Map:** *No. 48.*

Approach
Take the B847 Kinloch Rannoch to Trinafour road. The road crosses a dried up burn, the Allt na Moine Buidhe. A few yards past it a track runs up the hillside and leads to a small catchment dam. Leave the car here.

Ascent Route
Ascend the burn to a plateau from which the summit is visible ahead. If there is good snow cover, ascend by means of the south ridge, otherwise ascend via the corrie to its head and turn back to the summit.

Descent Route
As for ascent.

Variant

The north face offers broad gentle slopes that hold the snow well and may be a useful practice ground.

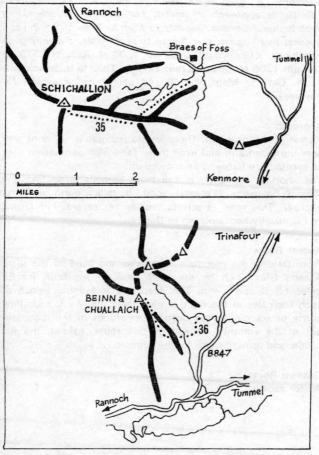

37 Beinn a'Ghlo
3671 ft.

Character: *A magnificent isolated and complex mountain, difficult to approach in winter, but offering superb skiing opportunities.* **Season:** *January to March.* **Aspect:** *South-east.* **Access:** *Bus — poor. Car — poor to reasonable, depending on conditions. Kirkmichael.* **Dep. alt:** 1300 *ft.* **Ascent:** 2370 *ft.* **Ter. alt:** 1300 *ft.* **Downhill run:** 2370 *ft.* **Time to main summit:** 3½ *h.* **Cat:** 5. **Map:** *No.* 49 *(48 useful and essential for traverse).*

Approach
Access is the problem. There are no motorable rights of way near the mountain, and even those for which permission may be granted are liable to be snowed up.

The shortest approach to the main summit is to take the Gleann Fearnach (Fernate) road, 4 miles north of Kirkmichael. This road is private, but serves several hill farms, and is usually kept open up to Daldhu.

Ascent Route
From Daldhu the mountain dominates the head of the glen. Ascend Glen Loch by the north bank of the burn for 2½ miles till it opens out. The deep and forbidding trench of Loch Loch lies to the right, while ahead, due west, a shallow corrie peters out in the deep upper slopes of the mountain left of the summit. Ascend by this route, gaining the flat saddle and turning north for the summit.

Descent Route
As for ascent.

38 Beinn a'Ghlo
3505 ft.   Perthshire
(Braigh Coire Chruinn Bhalgain)

Character: *Magnificent ski terrain of great interest, not visible either from the road or nearby summits.* **Season:** *January to April.* **Aspect:** *South-west.* **Access:** *Bus — none. Car — fair. Blair Atholl.* **Dep. alt:** *1350 ft.* **Ascent:** *2250 ft.* **Ter. alt:** *1350 ft.* **Downhill run:** *2150 ft.* **Time to main summit:** *3½ h.* **Cat:** *4.* **Map:** *Nos. 48 and 49.* **Diag:** *R. 37.*

Approach
From Blair Atholl take the road up the Tilt signposted "Monzie", but when the road turns up the east side of Glen Fender, continue over the river Fender, and take the road that serves the small farms lying on the west side of Glen Fender. This terminates at Allt an Dulish. It may be necessary to leave the car a mile or so short due to the road not being snowploughed.

Ascent Route
Double S gully. Continue up the west side of Glen Fender, passing the burn that runs off Carn Liath, and continuing to the burn running out of the col between Carn Liath and the 3505 ft. top of Beinn a'Ghlo. This burn leads to the great hidden double-S shaped gully that runs S.W. from the summit. The burn may be followed all the way, or as the prospect opens up, variants used.

Descent Route
The build up of snow on this mountain is considerable, and will lie to one flank or another of the Double S gully depending on the winter. The gully and the burn below hold snow well, and should lead even in late season down to 1600 ft.

Variants
This route may also be taken from Marble Lodge (see R. 37). There is a stiff 800 ft. climb out of Glen Tilt. From the summit the main (3671 ft.) top of Beinn a'Ghlo is clearly visible to the E.N.E., and may be reached within an hour.

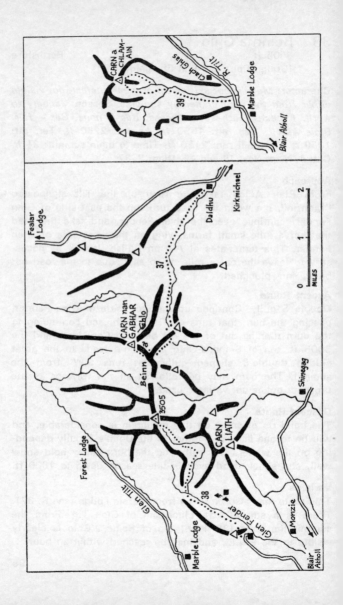

39 Carn a Chlamain (Croinidh)
3159 ft.

Character: *A fine top at the head of a superb snow corrie. Access route to some of Scotland's best langlauf country.* **Season:** *February to early April.* **Aspect:** *due South.* **Access:** *Bus — none. Car — excellent. Blair Atholl.* **Dep. alt:** *890 ft.* **Ascent:** *2270 ft.* **Ter. alt:** *890 ft.* **Downhill run:** *2270 ft.* **Time to main summit:** *3 h.* **Cat:** *4.* **Map:** *Nos. 48 and 37.* **Unnamed summit, G.R. map ref.** 915759.

Access
At Blair Atholl take the public road up Glen Tilt, taking the turning marked 'Old Blair' that crosses the river. Within 200 yd. of the bridge is a lodge at which permission should be sought to drive up Glen Tilt (alternative: apply Factor's house, Estate Office). Drive up to the keeper's house at Clach-ghlas just beyond the little cottage known as Marble Lodge.

Ascent Route
Croinidh Face. If the snow line is at road level, leave the car on the north side of the river half a mile beyond Marble Lodge, and ascend the west side of the Allt Croinidh. After a steep beginning, a path of sorts leads into the south basin of the mountain. If the snow line is higher, drive to Clach-ghlas, and take the stalkers path that leads back to the Allt Croinidh (north side).

The south basin is a superb ski ground, and is best taken either on the extreme left, or by taking the basin in the middle, reaching the east ridge by a broad gully that leads out about 100 yd. east of the summit.

Descent Route
The easiest line runs off to the west, but the finest line drops right down the face. Beware of avalanche after fresh snow fall or moist wind.

G

This summit is unnamed in all but the 6 inch maps. The name shown is that given in the 6 inch map, but differs from the local name of 'Croinidh'.

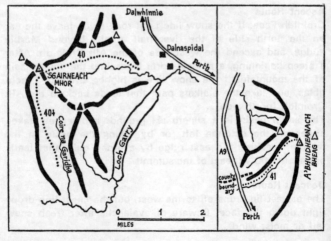

40 Sgairneach Mhor
3160 ft.

Character: *Long gentle snow slopes set amid immense landscapes.* **Season:** *January to April.* **Aspect:** *South and Northeast.* **Access:** *Bus — good. Car — excellent. Dalwhinnie.* **Dep. alt:** 1300 *ft.* **Ascent:** 1860 *ft. or* 3000 *ft.* **Ter. alt:** 1300 *ft.* **Downhill run:** 1860 *ft. or* 3000 *ft.* **Time to main summit:** 2½ *h.* **Cat:** 1 *or* 3. **Map:** *No. 48.*

Approach
Turn off the A9 Perth to Kingussie road 100 yd. south of Dalnaspidal station. A track crosses the railway line by a level crossing and runs to the west side of Loch Garry. Park at the second bridge, half a mile from the main road.

Ascent Route
Ascend directly towards the summit up the north (right) flank of the Allt Coire Luidhearnaidh. The burn veers S.W., leading to a snow bowl and a shallow col. As one approaches the col, turn north and head directly for the summit.

Descent Route
The simplest and speediest route is that of the ascent. But to do so would be to miss the great opportunities of this massif, for a superb snow bowl lies due south of the summit, offering runs of two miles or more.

From the summit ski due south holding Mam Ban on one's right, and entering the long gentle Coire na Garidha. Bearing in mind that every foot descended has later to be ascended, continue as long as wished.

The re-ascent should aim for Meallan Buidhe, a rounded summit of about 2850 ft. due north of the corrie. Those looking for the technically easiest descent should now ski into the corrie for the original ascent. The finest way off (Cat: 3) is to hold to the spur called Ceann Gorm which leads directly to the starting point.

Variation

It is possible to continue right down the Coire na Garidha to its base, contour eastwards, and gain the path down Loch Garry. This involves minimum extra climbing, and superb ski running, but a four mile walk back.

41 A'Bhuidheanach Bheag
3064 ft.
Perthshire

Character: *Easy and much finer than it looks from the road.*
Season: *January to April.* **Aspect:** *South.* **Access:** *Bus or car; unrivalled for ease of access. Dalwhinnie.* **Dep. alt:** 1400 *ft.*
Ascent: 1600 *ft.* **Ter. alt:** 1400 *ft.* **Downhill run:** 1600 *ft.*
Time to main summit: 1½ *h.* **Cat:** 1. **Map:** *No. 37.*

Approach
Stop the car at the first stream north of the Perthshire-Inverness-shire county boundary on the A9 from Perth to Kingussie.

Ascent Route
Follow the burn, then the shoulder to its north to reach the summit.

Descent Route
At will on the upper section, but the ascent route lower down.

42 Carn na Caim

Character: *Both broad easy slopes and narrow constricted skiing.* **Season:** *January to March, even April on occasion.* **Aspect:** *North-west.* **Access:** *Bus none, car — excellent. Dal. whinnie.* **Dep. alt:** 1270 *ft.* **Ascent:** 1800 *ft.* **Ter. alt:** 1270 *ft.* **Downhill run:** 1800 *ft.* **Time to main summit:** 2¼ *h.* **Cat:** 2. **Map:** No. 37.

Approach
Park the car by the A9 at the Wade Bridge, a mile and a quarter south of Dalwhinnie.

Ascent Route
Follow the general line of the Allt Coire Uilleim. In the upper basin trend left (north). After a severe thaw it may be necessary to hold to the right where the snow collects better. From the lip of the basin the summit lies a mile to the north.

Descent Route
As for ascent. On the Allt Uilleim hold to the south bank. In the middle part of the route the skiing may be over the stream bed, and very constricted.

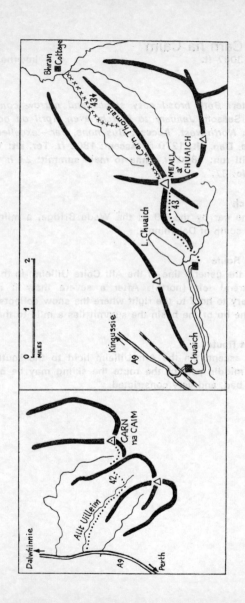

43 Meall Chuaich traverse
3120 ft.

Character: *Holds the snow very well despite its low altitude. An interesting mountain and delightful traverse.* **Season:** *January to April.* **Aspect:** *North.* **Access:** *Bus — none. Car — good. Dalwhinnie or Kingussie.* **Dep. alt:** *1300 ft.* **Ascent:** *1820 ft.* **Ter. alt:** *1200 ft.* **Downhill run:** *1920 ft.* **Time to main summit:** *2¼ h.* **Cat:** 3. **Map:** *No. 37.*

Approach
Turn off the A9 Perth to Kingussie road 3 miles north of Dalwhinnie. This turning is not easily seen but leads to the railway cottages at Cuaich, the access road passing first over the river, then under the railway. Here permission should be sought to use the road built to serve the Hydro Board culvert running from Loch Cuaich. Drive to the loch (hut).

Ascent Route
From the hut take a direct line to the summit by way of the south face of the mountain.

Descent Route
The N.N.W. face of the peak holds snow exceptionally well, and is a landmark seen from the upper Spey valley. The objective is to reach Bhran cottage in Glen Tromie. The problem is the shoulder known as Carn Thomais, which is a peat hag and is flanked by very high heather. The natural line of descent will take one down to the Allt na Feinnich, which is the best line late in the season. One then has a walk of two miles to Bhran cottage, with a diversion up or downstream to find a bridge. If the snow is low enough in the gullies, trend east from Carn Thomais to enter the Allt na Fearna, cross it, and follow its side to meet the Tromie (bridge).

If being collected by car it is well to remember that Glen Tromie is private, and permission should be obtained at the keeper's cottage to drive up the glen, but it is unrestricted up to Glen Tromie Lodge.

44　Beinn Dearg
3304 ft.

Perthshire

Character: *A fine peak of great interest to the skier.* **Season:**
*In terms of snow, January to April, but approaches often
blocked till mid March.* **Aspect:** *South.* **Access:** *Bus — none.
Car — good, if access roads open, otherwise poor. Calvine.*
Dep. alt: 1600 *ft.* **Ascent:** 1700 *ft.* **Ter. alt:** 1600 *ft.* **Downhill
run:** 1700 *ft.* **Cat:** 4. **Map:** *Nos. 48 (approach), 37 (mountain).*

Approach
From A9, leave road at Calvine along a very rough road
marked 'Minigaig Pass'. This is a private road of the Atholl
Estates, from whom permission should be sought (Factor's
House, Blair Atholl).
The road runs 7 miles to Bruar Lodge, a fine sheltered
situation under Beinn Dearg.

Ascent Route
Immediately behind the Lodge a shoulder rises to the N.E.,
and forms the route of ascent. At 2500 ft. it eases off, the
summit lies E.N.E., and is taken direct.

Descent Route
As for ascent. The upper slopes are broad and capable of
great variation. It is important to hold to the spur above
Bruar Lodge for the descent. Not only does it give excellent
skiing, but unlike neighbouring spurs, provides more continuous snow.

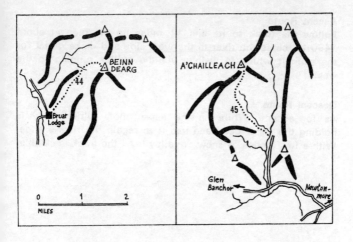

45　A'Chailleach
3045 ft.

Inverness-shire

Character: *Broad gentle slopes and an easy summit.* **Season:** *January to March.* **Aspect:** *East.* **Access:** *Bus — none. Car — good. Newtonmore.* **Dep. alt:** *1200 ft.* **Ascent:** *1900 ft.* **Downhill run:** *1400 ft. (1600 ft.).* **Time to main summit:** *2½ h.* **Cat:** *1.* **Map:** *No. 37.*

Approach
From Newtonmore take the Glen Banchor road for two miles to the point marked 'private road' (turning place). The road continues over the Allt a Chaoruinn to the farms in the upper valley. A car track, barely discernible at the outset, rises from behind the turning place and runs up the hillside beside the Allt a Chaoruinn. It is not shown on the map. One may drive up this a further 200 ft. or more depending on the vehicle.

Ascent Route
Follow the track to its end 1½ miles up the glen at about 1450 ft., cross the river to the west side and make direct for the summit which is visible, via the gullies running to the west.

Descent Route
As for ascent. While on the ascent note which gully is holding the snow best, and use it to regain the river's edge. With a few inches of snow at valley level the track is skiable.

46   Sgoran Dubh Mor
3635 ft.   Inverness-shire
Sgor Gaoith
3658 ft.

Character: *Magnificent ski terrain of great variety.* **Season:** *December to April.* **Aspect:** *West.* **Access:** *Bus — none. Car — good.* **Dep. alt:** 1050 *ft.* **Ascent:** 2500 *ft.* **Downhill run:** 1900 *ft.* **Time to main summit:** 3 *h.* **Cat:** 3. **Map:** *No. 37, or Cairngorms Tourist map.*

Approach
From Feshie Bridge (B970, Insh to Rothiemurchus) take the road up the east side of Glen Feshie. A mile and a half after reaching the flat part of the Glen (airstrip) take the rough road up the north side of the Allt Ruadh. This is just before reaching Balachroick House.

Ascent Route

Cross the locked gate into the Cairngorm Nature Reserve, and follow the excellent car track to its end, taking the lowest of any junctions. Here at 1500 ft. the forest ends, and the spur of Meall Tionail stands directly ahead. Gain the neck between Meall Tionail and point 3185 ft., via Coire na Cloiche, and then on rising traverse going due east reach the col between that point and the summit ridge of the Sgoran Dubh. One now has the choice of an ascent northwards to Sgoran Dubh Mor (3635 ft.) or southwards to the more shapely and higher Sgor Gaoith (3658 ft.). To gain Sgoran Dubh (the best ski run) make an ascending traverse of the wide upper slopes of the Allt a Mharcaidh to reach the west spur of the summit ridge. For Sgorr Gaoith, one must first reach the main ridge, then proceed south along it to the summit.

Descent Route

From Sgoran Dubh, follow the route of descent to the col. If there is ample snow in Coire na Cloiche, one can ski back to the neck, and descend the corrie, from which a snow band runs right down to the Allt Ruadh (1500 ft.). One can check its continuity on the ascent. Otherwise descend from the col into the basin of the Allt a Chram-altain. These are wider and more interesting slopes, but terminate higher (1700 ft.) and further from the starting point.

From Sgor Gaoith, a direct descent leads onto steep slopes in Cat: 4. These slopes lead down to the Allt a Chram altain. One can however find gentler terrain by returning to the col, and descending by Coire na Cloiche.

47 Carn Ban Mor
3443 ft.

Character: *A most accessible peak offering fine easy skiing, and access to great snowfields.* **Season:** *December to late April.* **Aspect:** *West.* **Access:** *Bus — none. Car — good.* **Dep. alt:** *1100 ft.* **Ascent:** *2350 ft.* **Ter. alt:** *1100 ft.* **Downhill run:** *2350 ft.* **Time to main summit:** *2 h.* **Cat:** *2.* **Map:** *No. 37, or Cairngorms Tourist map.* **Diag:** *R. 46.*

Approach
From the B970 east Speyside road from Kingussie to Rothie-murchus, take the Glen Feshie branch at Feshie Bridge. It is sign-posted 'Achlean'. Proceed up the glen for 5 miles to the end of the metalled road and park at Achlean cottage. A good path leads directly to the summit of the mountain.

Ascent Route
Follow the line of the path. Above about 2500 ft. it will almost certainly be obliterated, and it is best to keep to the crown of the west ridge leading to the summit.

Descent Route
The west side holds a great deal of snow late in the season. The longest runs in late season generally lie on the far (Coire Gorm) side of the corrie, but the best opportunities can be easily assessed during the ascent.

48 Monadh Mor
3651 ft.

Character: *Easy skiing but only for those with a knowledge of mountains.* **Season:** *January to April.* **Aspect:** *West.* **Access:** *Bus — none. Car — good. Kingussie.* **Dep. alt:** 1100 *ft.* **Ascent:** 3300 *ft.* **Ter. alt:** 1100 *ft.* **Downhill run:** 3300 *ft.* **Time to main summit:** 4 *h.* **Cat:** 3, *but very remote.* **Map:** *No. 37, or Cairngorms Tourist map.* **Diag:** *R. 46.*

Approach
As for R. 47.

Ascent Route
Follow R. 47 for Carn Ban Mor. It is not necessary to make the actual summit, though it is worth doing so. The col to the south is adequate. To the east lies the great sloping plateau of the Moine Mhor, or great moss. Monadh Mor rises beyond. Ski E.S.E. to a hollow in the plateau just north of point 3009, pass through a shallow col, and drop into the head of the Allt Luineag. From here the summit lies S.E. and 800 ft. above, gained via the 3326 ft. top.

Descent Route
As far as Carn Ban Mor, the route is the same. From there to Achlean there are a number of well filled gullies which last well into late spring, any one of which may be taken.

Traverse
Cat: 5. From the summit of Monadh Mor, instead of returning to Carn Ban Mor, ski due north to meet the Allt Luineag (almost certainly snowed in and invisible), re-ascend to 2600 ft. and descend to Glen Einich by Coire Dhondail. This is a steep magnificent snow corrie, and should not be tackled if there is risk of avalanche, or in hard snow. As an alternative to the long carry down Glen Einich to Coylumbridge, cross the Einich burn half a mile down-stream of the loch,

and ascend the north spur of the Sgoran Dubh to point 2565 ft. (ascent of 900 ft.), from which point one may ski down the Allt a Mharcaidh. The end of this run through open pine-wood is exceptionally beautiful. A car can be driven to the foot of this wood by taking the forestry road running north-east from the Feshie road at Blackmill.

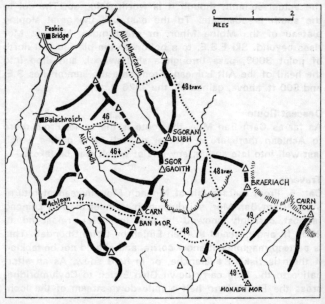

49 Cairn Toul
4241 ft.   Inverness-shire

Character: *One of the finest and remotest ski-peaks in Scotland.* **Season:** *January to May.* **Aspect:** *South-west.* **Access:** *Bus — none. Car — good. Kingussie.* **Dep. alt:** 1100 *ft.* **Ascent:** 3950 *ft.* **Ter. alt:** 1100 *ft.* **Downhill run:** 3950 *ft.* **Time to main summit:** 5 *h.* **Cat:** 3. **Map:** *Nos.* 37, 41, *or Cairngorms Tourist map.* **Diag:** *R.* 46.

Approach
As for Carn Ban Mor, R. 47.

Ascent Route
WARNING — This route involves several hours on a plateau totally exposed to the weather, with little shelter to withdraw to that is not in itself exceptionally remote. It should only be undertaken by a strong party with knowledge of navigation in misty conditions.

Ascend to summit of Carn Ban Mor (R. 47) and ski down the gentle plateau in a E.S.E. direction to reach the lochan just north of point 3009 ft. The summit lies due east, three miles distant. Do not make directly for it, but rather for a point a mile or so to the N.W. of it, using the right hand branch of the Allt Luineag as the route of ascent. Near the apparent crest strike eastwards to reach the true crest at the summit. This route is chosen so that in the event of mist coming down the skier will have a good guide to his route of descent.

Descent Route
As for route of ascent.

Traverse
There is an opportunity here for one of the great traverses in the Cairngorms. From the summit descend by the Allt Clais an-t Sabhail into Glen Geusachan, from which one may reach Derry Lodge (2 h.) or Corrour Bothy (shelter — ¾ h.).

The bothy may be more directly gained by leaving the summit in a southerly direction and dipping into Coire Odhar and dropping directly upon Corrour Bothy (Cat: 5). One can camp the night at Corrour, and move up or down the Larig Ghru next day, to reach Aviemore or Braemar. See also the traverse in R. 48.

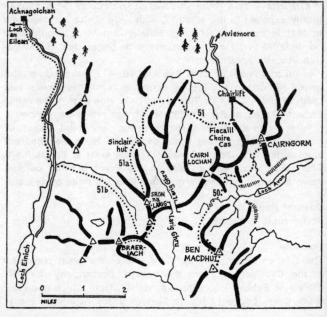

50 Ben Macdui (North Side)
4300 ft.
Aberdeenshire

Character: *Second highest peak in British Isles, and a superb viewpoint. Easy skiing on plateau terrain, but remote. Dangerous in bad weather or mist.* **Season:** *February to May.* **Aspect:** *North.* **Access:** *Bus and car — exceptionally good. Aviemore.* **Dep. alt:** *3500 ft.* **Ascent:** *1900 ft.* **Ter. alt:** *1750 ft.* **Downhill run:** *2850 ft.* **Time to main summit:** *3 h.* **Cat:** *2 (Fiacaill Choire Cas, 3).* **Map:** *No. 41, or Cairngorms Tourist map.*

Approach
From Aviemore (station, A9) take bus or car to the Cairngorm car park, then the chairlift to the top station (2500 ft.).

Ascent Route
Ascend Cairngorm carrying skis ($\frac{1}{2}$ h.). Ben Macdui may now be seen, with two intervening spurs. One can see where the snow accumulation is best, and choose the best line.

The summit of Cairngorm is rocky. To find the best snowfield walk about 50 yards due south from the summit and then ski down to upper Coire Raibert. The greater the descent, the greater the subsequent re-ascent on to the spur running back from Coire an-t-Sneachda. Do not hold too close to the Loch Avon side of this spur. The best line is about 200 yd. from the lip of Coire an-t-Sneachda. A further short descent leads onto the south slopes of Cairn Lochain. Ascend the south spur of that peak some hundred or more feet below the summit level. Ahead now lies a gently undulating plateau with the cone of the North top of Ben Macdui (4244 ft.) directly beyond. It is best passed on the left. The main summit lies 20 min. beyond, with a slight dip in between.

H

Descent Route

As for the ascent as far as Coire Raibert. From here reach the summit of the Fiacaill Choire Cas, and descend its narrow upper rib. At the first opportunity drop into the upper bowl of Coire Cas, which leads to the pistes.

Variation

A faster route of descent to the valley is gain the shoulder running N.W. from the summit of Cairn Lochain. Crossing this leads to a shallow snow bowl — the Lurcher's burn (Allt Creag an Leth-Choin), which can be descended directly to the Allt Mor where one may rejoin the ski road to Cairngorm.

51 Braeriach
4248 ft.
Inverness-shire

Character: *A superb mountain of high altitude with the most extensive snowfields in Scotland.* **Season:** *January to May.* **Aspect:** *North.* **Access:** *Bus — none. Car — moderate. Aviemore.* **Dep. alt:** *(a) 3200 ft. (b) 925 ft.* **Ascent:** *(a) 2600 ft. (b) 3300 ft.* **Ter. alt:** *(a) 1250 ft. (b) 925 ft.* **Time to main summit:** *(a) 3½ h. (b) 4½ h.* **Cat:** *(a) 4. (b) 3.* **Map:** *Nos. 41 (or 38) and 37, or Cairngorms Tourist map.* **Diag:** *R. 50.*

Approach

The remoteness of this peak is both its drawback and attraction.

(a)　Take the car to Cairngorm car park and take the Fiacaill lift to the base of the Fiacaill Choire Cas (3200 ft.).

(b)　From Rothiemurchus take the road to Loch an Eilean, and continue along the rough car track on the north side to the locked gate at the entrance to Glen Einich, just south of Achnagoichan.

114

Ascent Route

(a)   Descend on a traverse line in the direction of Loch Morlich. Cross the Allt a Creag an Leth-Choin, and trend west holding one's height to penetrate the ridge of Creag an Leth-Choin at Creag a Chalamain gap. The Larig Ghru lies below, and beyond its burn, a small hut (Sinclair Hut). From the hut ascend steep heathery hillsides for 300 ft. to reach the plateau at the base of Coire Gorm, one of the finest skiing corries in Scotland. Ascend it to the summit of Sron na Larig, and follow the ridge round the head of Coire Beannaidh to the summit.

(b)   Ascend the road up Glen Einich for 4 miles to the point where the Beanaidh Beag (river) joins the Einich (1550 ft.). The river leads in by wide slopes to Coir Beannaidh which should be followed to its head, where it forms a col between Sron na Larig and the summit, which is one mile west of the col.

Descent Route

Both routes as for ascent. Note that between the summit and the Beannaidh col there is a narrow section of ridge, and the route is not suited to windy or white-out conditions.

N.B. Route (a) is not suitable if a general snow cover is not lying down to 1500 ft.

52   Ben Macdui
4300 ft.   Aberdeenshire

Character: *Interesting skiing on highly varied terrain on the second highest peak in the country.* **Season:** *February to April.* **Aspect:** *South.* **Access:** *Bus — none. Car — poor, but depending on development of access situation could improve (1970).* *Make inquiries at Mar Lodge, Braemar.* **Dep. alt:** 1350 *ft.* **Ascent:** 3000 *ft.* **Ter. alt:** 1350 *ft.* **Downhill run:** 3000 *ft.* **Time to main summit:** 3½ *h.* **Cat:** 3. **Map:** *No.* 41.

Approach

Till recently (1969) it was possible to obtain a key for the locked gate at the mouth of Glen Derry, and so drive to Derry Lodge. The charge was £1. This facility has now been withdrawn, and it is rarely possible to get permission to drive to the Lodge. The only practicable way to get a day's skiing now is to use a bicycle or motor cycle. With a bicycle it is often possible to go two miles beyond Derry Lodge when there is no snow at this level.

Ascent Route

From Derry Lodge take the path up Glen Luibeg to the spur at the foot of Sron Riach. This spur leads to the main summit of the mountain.

Descent Route

On the ascent the huge southern snowfields of Macdui will have been visible. Two descents are possible. If Sron Riach carries a good snow wreath, which is usual, it provides an exhilirating descent. Equally the south gully that drops in Allt Carn a Mhaim can be a superb steep (Cat: 4) run. The remainder of the return is as for the ascent.

53 Beinn a Bhuird (South Top)
3860 ft.   Aberdeenshire

Character: *A superb snow-holding hill, offering great diversity of skiing.* **Season:** *January to May.* **Aspect:** *South-east.* **Access:** *Bus — none. Car — poor. Land Rover — exceptional. This terrain is being opened up, and access may improve. Mar Lodge Hotel is anxious to encourage skiers and may give permission to take a Land Rover up the track that runs to the summit of the mountain. Braemar.* **Dep. alt:** 1350 ft., *at Invercauld or Linn of Quoich.* **Ascent:** 2800 ft. — 2600 ft. **Ter. alt:** 1350 ft. **Downhill run:** 2400 ft. — 2200 ft. **Time to main summit:** 3¾ — 4 h. **Cat:** 2. **Map:** No. 41.

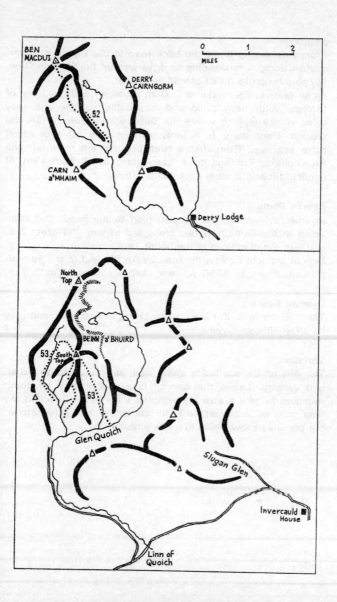

Approach

From Invercauld, enter the back road to the Castle at Invercauld Bridge. It is possible to drive well up the Slugain Glen, but permission to do so should be sought.

From Mar Lodge, take the Glen Quoich road at Linn of Quoich. With permission and a suitable vehicle one may drive all the way to where the Dubh Gleann burn enters the Quoich. Here there is a ford, suitable only for four-wheel drive vehicles. Thereafter a road ascends the mountain via An Diollaid. Timings have been given as if from Linn of Quoich: bicycle a most useful alternative.

Ascent Route

Invercauld: Ascend the Slugain glen to the head, and drop down to the Quoich water, cross and ascend the great S.E. corrie of the mountain to the South Top.

Linn of Quoich: Follow the road by An Diollaid to the summit plateau. When at 3700 ft. veer east to gain the South Top.

Descent Route

The S.E. corrie is the finest open skiing in Scotland, and may be taken almost anywhere.

Variation

The Allt na Beinne holds snow well, and provides an excellent descent. Leave the summit in a slightly east of south direction to gain a steadily steeping snow bowl. Descend the final gully on the west flank. In late spring it is very narrow, but provides snow down to a low altitude.

54 Morven

2862 ft.

Character: *A simple isolated conical hill in a snow bearing area.* **Season:** *January to March.* **Aspect:** *East.* **Access:** *Bus – none. Car – good. Dinnet.* **Dep. alt:** *(a) 750 ft. (b) 1250 ft.* **Ascent:** *(a) 2170 ft. (b) 1620 ft.* **Ter. alt:** *(a) 750 ft. (b) 1250 ft.* **Downhill run:** *(a) 2100 ft. (b) 1620 ft.* **Cat:** 1. **Map:** *No. 39.*

Approach

(a)   From Dinnet or Tarland take the A94 at Milton of Logie as far as Newkirk; Morven is due west. Follow the farm road to Bridgefoot.

(b)   From Bridge of Gairn follow Glen Gairn as far as Lary Farm (3 miles), from where a hill road rises to Morven Lodge. Park at about the 1250 ft. contour. This road is likely to be blocked if the snow line is low.

Ascent Route

(a)   Ascend on the line of the Coinlach burn to the summit by the south-east flank.

(b)   From a convenient point on the Morven Lodge road cross the Lary burn and head for the summit by its S.W. flank.

Descent Route

Both, as for ascent.

55 Bidean an Eoin Dearg

3430 ft.

Character: *Unlikely but stimulating ski terrain in a West Highland setting.* **Season:** *February to March.* **Aspect:** *North (variation, South).* **Access:** *Car – good. Bus – none.* **Dep. alt:** *1100 ft.* **Ascent:** *2650 ft.* **Ter. alt:** *1100 ft.* **Downhill run:** *2650 ft.* **Cat:** 3. **Map:** *No. 26.*

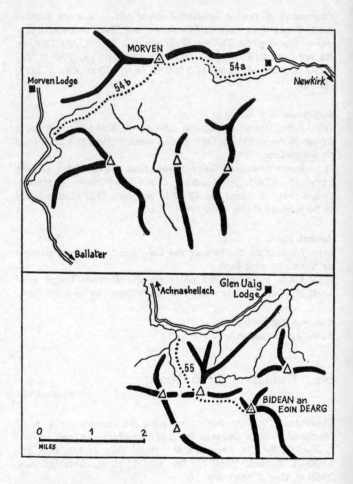

Approach

From the A890, Achnasheen to Strome road, take the forestry road to the south-east at Craig, 2 miles east of Achnashellach Lodge. The road has a locked gate above the tree line, and permission to use the road should be sought from the keeper at Craig. Ascend the road, which runs up the Allt a Chonais towards a bothy marked Glenuaig Lodge. Park at a point due north of Sgurr a Chaorachain, 2 miles from the bothy.

Ascent Route

Cross the Pollon Buidhe burn and ascend due south. An initial steep section of grass, over which skis will usually be carried, takes one to the lip of a fine corrie not apparent from below nor from the map. Fine varied snow slopes lead up to the summit of Sgurr a Chaorachain. From this summit immense south facing snow slopes run down towards the head of Loch Monar, but have, of course, later to be re-ascended. The route suggested here is to descend eastwards to make the col with Bidean an Eoin Dearg.

Descent Route

Return by the route of ascent.

Variation

Bidean an Eoin Dearg has three deeply set snow-holding bays to its north. One may be reached by a ridge that abuts onto the summit plateau, thus providing a different descent. However, unless the snow line is at 1500 ft., there is a long walk back to the car.

56   Beinn Iutharn Mhor
3424 ft.

Character: *A singularly remote mountain, making a fine culmination to a long gentle approach.* **Season:** *February to March.* **Aspect:** *North-east.* **Access:** *Car — excellent. Blairgowrie or Braemar.* **Dep. alt:** *3000 ft.* **Ascent:** *2000 ft.* **Ter. alt:** *2200 ft.* **Downhill run:** *3100 ft.* **Time to main summit:** *4 h.* **Cat:** *3.* **Map:** *No. 41.*

Approach
Drive to Cairnwell chairlift at the head of Glen Shee.

Ascent Route
From the top of the Cairnwell chairlift, descend to Loch Vrotachan and continue past on an eastward descent to reach the Baddoch burn that flows northwards to Glen Cluanie. This is featureless country, and the tour should not be made in misty conditions. Ascend the Baddoch burn till just below the nameless burn entering from the east at national grid reference: 098787 (2000 ft.). This burn is identifiable by the fact that where it enters the Baddoch burn it cuts into the ground deeply, and in winter forms a snowy gorge. Gain the bed of the burn about half a mile from its junction with the Baddoch burn, at which point it is a broad U-shaped trench, superb for skiing, and remarkably sheltered from the wind. Follow its many contortions (always in an eastwardly direction) till it suddenly peters out at 2500 ft. Ahead now is Beinn Iutharn Bheag, and northwards a valley drops gently towards Inverey. An Socach is directly to the north. Holding an E.S.E. course, make a gentle ascending traverse towards a bay in the hills to the east under Beinn Iutharn Bheag in which nestles Loch nan Eun. Gain the north end of this loch, and then traverse steeply uphill on the east flank of Beinn Iutharn Bheag to reach a col at 2700 ft. between Beinn Iutharn Mhor and Mam nan Carn. From this col one looks across to Beinn Iutharn Mhor, and the superb snow-holding N.E.

corrie of the mountain. Make an ascending traverse round the shallow headwall, initially south-east, then east again to reach the col between Beinn Iutharn Mhor and Mam nan Carn. The summit slopes are straightforward and run in a N.N.W. direction.

Descent Route
As for ascent as far as Baddoch burn, then ascend past Loch Vrotachan to the shoulder of the Cairnwell and onto the pistes of Butchart's corrie.

N.B. In view of the length of the route, and the 700 foot re-ascent from Baddoch burn, allow ample time, say 2½ h., for the return to the car from the summit.

57 Aonach Mor
3999 ft.

Character: *A huge brute of a mountain with a vast gentle western corrie.* **Season:** *February to April.* **Aspect:** *West.* **Access:** *Bus — none. Car — poor.* **Dep. alt:** *600 ft.* **Ascent:** *3400 ft.* **Ter. alt:** *600 ft.* **Downhill run:** *2500 ft.* **Time to main summit:** *3 h.* **Cat:** *1.* **Map:** *Nos. 36 (approach), 47 (mountain), or Ben Nevis and Glencoe Tourist map.*

Approach
Branch off the A82 Fort William to Speanbridge road at Torlundy, and follow the forestry road marked 'Leanachan Forest'. Look ahead and to the right for the 2172 ft. summit of Sgurr Finnisgaig. After about 2½ miles, when almost abreast of it, a branch track turns south towards it and Aonach Mor. It leads to the Aluminium Company service railway.

Ascent Route

Heavy going up hillsides, at first wooded, eventually leads to easier and more open slopes. The long shallow western corrie lies before one. Significantly it is called Allt an Sneachda, the burn of the snow. Ascend to the first top. The main summit is half a mile beyond.

Descent Route

As for route of ascent.

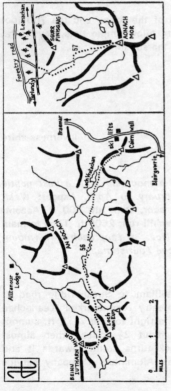

Index of Summits

125

Illustrations

Illustrations

2

3

4

5

6

7

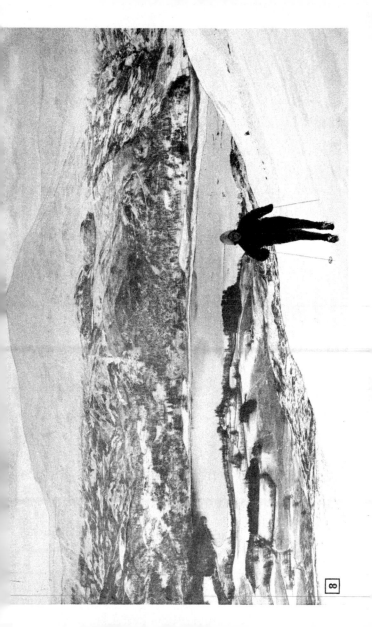

8